4

Industry
and
Social
Life

Industry
and
Social
Life

EDWARD GROSS

University of Minnesota

WM. C. BROWN COMPANY PUBLISHERS

135 SOUTH LOCUST STREET • DUBUQUE, IOWA 52003

Manufactured by WM. C. BROWN CO. INC., Dubuque, Iowa
Printed in U. S. A.

PREFACE

THE impacts of industrialization upon society are important and challenging in all industrial and would-be industrial nations. These impacts, forces and relationships are simultaneously troublesome and stimulating, not only to the persons involved, but to scholars as well. Researchers from various disciplines have sought to analyze numerous facets of industrialization and its concommitant social adjustments. One of the key issues of our times is concerned with our ability to mesh technological and social systems, structures, and organizations.

Fortunately we have much more knowledge of these relationships than we had just two decades ago. This expansion in knowledge is a resultant of numerous studies dealing with selected aspects of relations between industrialization and socialization. These studies utilize a variety of approaches and techniques. They represent many fragments of knowledge, but to go from knowledge to understanding, these analytical pieces must be given synthesis — combined into a meaningful system and structure.

In this book, Professor Edward Gross has provided a critical comparative synthesis which in effect brings together for the first time the contributions of sociology to the newly emerging discipline of industrial relations. The volume would be of great value if only for the cataloguing and classification of diverse references in a single work. That, however, is not its major contribution. Instead the volume obtains its significance from the author's ability to make sense out of a mass of findings, selecting the meaningful and consequential, and provide a substantive, interpretive pattern of relationships. The whole is indeed more

v

than the sum of its parts, and represents new, provocative and insightful generalizations. The book provides new ways of thinking about these relationships and, through careful comparative analysis and synthesis, is pregnant with added understanding for the researcher and the practitioner. It is a unique and solid contribution to improved understanding in industrial relations.

As such, the Industrial Relations Center is pleased to have this book by Professor Gross as the third volume in its special book series published by the Wm. C. Brown Company. The two previous volumes in this series are *Development and Use of Weighted Application Blanks,* by George W. England, and *The Identification of Management Potential* by Thomas A. Mahoney, Thomas H. Jerdee, and Allan N. Nash.

Professor Gross is a staff member of the Industrial Relations Center, a member of the Sociology Department, and a member of the graduate faculty in Industrial Relations at the University of Minnesota. His contributions and publications in the areas of work, social organization, and the sociology of professions are well known. His ability to significantly relate industrial sociology and industrial relations will be apparent to those who read this volume.

This volume, like the others in the IRC series, seeks to explain and illuminate significant concepts in comparatively few pages. The evidence is carefully presented and evaluated, and appropriate conclusions are drawn. For the reader who wants to pursue a subject in more detail, the book has numerous references. It should be of special interest to students in sociology, industrial relations, and indeed all of the social sciences. Students in natural sciences, in engineering and the other professions will find much in this volume that will be helpful, surprising, and perhaps disturbing. Researchers will find new insights and stimuli.

Perhaps the book's greatest value will be for practitioners, who have not had time or opportunity, or just have not known how, to keep up with the tremendous number of studies encompassed in this volume. All managers, and industrial relations practitioners — and those in the professions — who seek to maintain and increase their competence through increased understanding and to prevent their own technological obsolescence, will find this volume a rewarding and enjoyable experience. It will stimulate new insights into not only old problems but into the ever increasingly urgent new problems that industrialization continues to pose for our society.

The present volume is not a cookbook with all of the answers to solutions to all of the problems of industry and society. It does, however, provide penetrating insights into these problems. Such insights can perhaps help us more from knowledge to understanding and wisdom at a time when these are sorely and urgently needed in relationships between industry and society.

Herbert G. Heneman, Jr.
Director, Industrial Relations Center.

CONTENTS

Contents

INTRODUCTION

THIS book represents an attempt to fill a gap in the literature on industrial relations. On the one hand, there already exist a number of excellent texts which serve to introduce the student to the field, acquaint him with the basic issues, and familiarize him with the major studies. On the other hand, the recent literature in the field is growing at a very rapid rate and being published in diverse journals, proceedings, and mimeographed collections. The mature student of industrial relations will not find either of these sources completely satisfying. A reading of basic texts often leaves one with an impression of tidiness and neatness that is really not the whole truth, by any means. On the other hand anyone who attempts to follow the current literature will get just the opposite impression — one of chaos — and that is not the whole truth either.

The goal of this work was to produce a volume — as short and compressed as possible — which would represent a second-level work for the person (academic or not, student or professional) who already had some familiarity with industrial relations but who wished to participate in the current debate and discussion in the field, at least to the extent of understanding and following that debate and discussion. Such a person will find that the distinctive characteristic of recent studies, apart from their sheer number, is their empirical character; hence the strongly empirical character of this book and the extensive referencing employed. At the same time, the researches reported are presented in a context of the main issues in the study of industrial relations — work and leisure, alienation, legitimation of managerial power, the costs of organization in human terms, to cite some examples.

Lastly it is necessary to emphasize the fact that the author is a sociologist, and the book reflects the preoccupation of that field with the social aspects of industrial relations. As the reader will soon see, however, that perspective quickly leads one at least into the outskirts of neighboring fields, such as the other social sciences and the applied disciplines of personnel and labor relations, management, and administration.

I wish to thank Mr. John Rollins for a major assistance in preparing the index.

Industrial Relations Center, University of Minnesota,
Minneapolis.
September, 1964.   Edward Gross.

CHAPTER 1

IMAGES OF MAN
IN SOCIETY

A man usually thinks of his work as a means to other ends. It is by means of his work that he earns a living, sends his children to college, takes a vacation, or saves for the future. Work has far wider effects than these, however, for what a man does for a living affects much of his life and makes up an important part of his identity. It is claimed that the same engineer took care of the waterworks of Paris before, during, and after the French Revolution, thereby providing an example of a kind of work that enables a man to stand apart from the world in which he lives. Such a case is quite exceptional, for the work that most persons do ties them closely to their fellows. A few persons do their work alone but most work, and certainly all the important work of the society, makes men come together in associations and organizations in order to do a better and more dependable job. Sometimes the organizations that result are enormously complex as in the case of modern industrialized nations, but even the shop committee or small work teams illustrate the same process.

Nor is that all. A man's work is an important key to his status. This is particularly so as his name and place of birth come to mean less and less in what they tell us about a man. When we ask a person to whom we have been newly introduced the question "What do you do?" he knows immediately that we are asking for the kind of work that he does. The answer he gives is important for it is our major means of placing the man in a scale of estimation. His answer

1

enables us to make a judgment of how much money he makes, where he lives, where he may work, what kinds of recreation he likes, and to what private clubs (if any) he belongs. As we make these estimates, our judgment of the man gradually takes shape. We decide whether he is a man we should respect or one we should avoid, whether we should take assistance from him or offer it to him, whether we want anything further to do with him or not. At the same time because we do make such estimates on the basis of a man's work, it becomes very important that these judgments be reliable. This in short, is what we are interested in in this book: Knowing what a man does for a living, what conclusions can we draw about him and with what degree of accuracy? In turn how does the work that persons do affect the broader social life of the society in which they live?

Work and Leisure

Different persons look at work in very different ways and particularly striking differences can be found at various points in history. The modern layman conceives of work as the way in which he makes his living or in terms of some use to which he expects to put his earnings; that is, he tells us about the *purpose* of his work. Such a view — one can call it "instrumental" — does not tell us what work itself is though it tells us why a man believes he is working. In any case, it is not the whole picture because work clearly serves other than instrumental functions. Morse and Weiss (1955) report on the results of asking a random national sample of employed men the following question: "If by some chance you inherited enough money to live comfortably without working, do you think that you would work anyway or not?" Eighty per cent responded that they would keep working anyhow. When asked why, most gave positive reasons such as "to keep occupied" and "keeps individual healthy, good for person," while some gave negative reasons such as references to the fact that without work they would "feel lost, go crazy," "feel bored," or "feel useless." Only six per cent referred to "habit" or "inertia" as reason for working. The authors reaffirm Durkheim's (1947 edition) and Freud's (1930, p. 34, note) observations when they state: "It is through the producing role that most men tie into society, and for this reason and others, most men find the producing role important for maintaining their sense of well-being." (Morse & Weiss, 1955, p. 198.) In a careful study of 678 white males of the "middle mass" (lower middle-class and upper working class) in Detroit, Wilensky (1961, b) finds that those with "orderly careers" (those showing some degree of predictability in job changes in the sense that one job was functional to performing the subsequent job and the second was of higher prestige) were those who participated most in both formal associations and primary relationships. Studies of the effects of loss of work owing to unemployment and retirement tend to bear out the general point of view of these studies. (Adams, 1939; Bakke, 1939; Caplow, 1955; Eisenberg & Lazarsfeld, 1938; Friedmann, 1961, pp. 126 and 128; Watson, 1942.)

However important to one's life organization work may be, one cannot conclude that the work will therefore be felt to be pleasant. Weiss and Kahn (1960) asked a sample of 371 employed Detroit men, over age 21, the question: "In your opinion, what makes the difference between something you would call work and something you would not call work?" Fifty-nine per cent described work as something performed because it is necessary rather than because it is enjoyed. Another 24 per cent said work was something involving payment or scheduling. In all, therefore, 83 per cent said work was something that either had to be done because of characteristics inherent in the task itself or was something assigned to one by someone else and paid for. From this point of view work is seen as ineluctably irksome. It is in this context that work is frequently contrasted with leisure (de Grazia, 1962, Chapters I and II; Moore, 1963, pp. 35-39; Tilgher, 1930). To the Greeks, leisure was the end of life in contrast to work which was the activity that slaves performed. For Aristotle leisure was essentially the practice of contemplation and the enjoyment of music. Plato asserted that whoever could not hold his place in the chorus was not really an educated man. To hold one's place meant to be able to sing and dance at the same time. With the Christian era, work was elevated somewhat but not greatly in value. To the Benedictines, work, especially if manual, had a certain purifying value: it helped in repentance or was a way of serving others. To St. Augustine, that work was best

3

which distracted one the least from divine contemplation. Such work might include hand labor, tilling, and small business. For St. Thomas work was necessary but if a man was fortunate enough to have a surplus of earthly goods so that he did not have to work, then he would certainly be under no obligation to do so. The great change in attitudes toward work came with the Renaissance, particularly among the Florentines: the world existed so that man might exhibit his mastery over it. The proper end of leisure, then, was not contemplation but the bending of nature to man's will. Hence the Renaissance leaders continually delight in work and sing its praises, a conception of work still connoted by the word "craftsman." In the eighteenth century, Adam Smith advanced the idea that an act is productive only if it makes a raw material into something useful for man. Work is the source of wealth. Such a concept is clearly related to Calvinist and Lutheran views of work as a way of serving God.

In the modern view leisure usually is treated as a residual category, as an activity in which one engages when one does not have to work. Work arises from the requirement that one cannot escape direct attention to the maintenance needs such as food, clothing, and shelter. One is at leisure when one is free from the need to be concerned about such needs. In earlier times this freedom might be purchased by a leisure class through slaves. In our own culture, it typically must be earned. Mead (1957, p. 13) thus points out that one works not only for the means by which one can enjoy free time but for the very right to enjoy it, a legacy, she feels, of Puritanism and of the Biblical conception of punishment for original sin. Engaging in any act for its expressive value only is suspect and must be earned. Here we have the complete contrast with the ancient view that work was degrading and in a class with bodily excretion (though equally necessary). Now leisure becomes suspect precisely because it is potentially enjoyable.

Such a sharp contrast — work as instrumental and leisure as the enjoyable — is, however, too rigid. Further the notion that leisure is somehow "free" time implies that it is free from constraint, a point of view which, as Berger (1962) notes, would make leisure almost an impossibility. He proposes instead that leisure be used to refer to those activities "whose normative content renders them most important to us, those things that we want to do for their own sake or those things that we feel ethically (as distinguished from expediently) constrained to do." (Berger, 1962, p. 38.) Indeed, it is precisely because the norms have been so completely internalized that persons are unaware of them and feel that they are acting freely without compulsion. Both work and leisure are controlled by norms. In the case of work the norms are instrumental, that is, they refer to those technical requirements that must be fulfilled in order to attain the goal for which work is being engaged in, whereas in the case of leisure, the norms are associated with a set of ultimate values which needs no further justification. It must be recognized, however, that work and leisure may change places even when so defined. Simmel (1950, p. 42) saw play as arising out of work when hunting for food turned into the fox hunt, and of course Veblen made similar observations. Eventually, Stone (1958, pp. 261-262) notes, we arrive at the spectacle in which one has pure play or the game carried out by professionals in which it is the players who are those who are working. Looked at in this way play becomes a major industry estimated to involve $30 billion a year and as having become part of the business relationship itself. Wolfenstein and Leites (1950, p. 21) call attention to the emergence of a "fun morality" in which fun is no longer merely permissible but becomes obligatory. If a person is not having fun, he feels ashamed or inadequate. Having fun then becomes a costly dead-serious business to the point where research grants are made to study the process of having fun. (Riesman, Potter, and Watson, 1960, a and b.)

Just as viewing play or leisure as a process of mere idling is inadequate, so it is inadequate to see work as only instrumental, as something that provides the necessaries only so that one is freed to play. As we have already noted, work has other functions in integrating the person into the society and is in fact engaged in for uses far beyond a living. "It is not physical hunger," writes Bell, "which is the driving force; there is a new hunger. The candied carrot, the desire for goods has replaced the stick; the standard of living has become a "built-in automatic drive." (Bell, 1960, p. 246.) When work is that important it becomes a major part of anyone's life though the amount of one's life or of one's week which is given

5

over to work is strangely variable between occupations (Wilensky, 1961, a). De Grazia (1962, p. 472) shows that in 1960 although farmers led all occupations in the average weekly hours spent by persons at work (52.0 hours), second in line were managers, officials, and proprietors (excluding farms) with an average of 49.5 hours whereas professional, technical, and kindred workers were third. By contrast, spending the smallest number of average weekly hours were laborers (excluding farm and mine) private household workers, and clerical workers. Whatever the explanations may be — and these figures certainly reflect part-time work and "involuntary leisure" — the paradoxical situation results in which the managers, executives, and professionals work the longest hours and become so wrapped up in their work that it is certainly foolish to limit the notion of work to the provision of the necessaries or to preparing for leisure.

In a strict sociological sense, work consists of group goal-directed activity. More generally, a work relationship can be defined as one in which two or more persons relate to each other in order to achieve a limited and definite goal or objective which is not necessarily identical with their personal goals. For the most part, the concern in industrial relations is with those kinds of goals which are economic. A group of persons meeting to arrange for a discussion of a community issue will find themselves related to each other in order to achieve a limited and definite goal, however, and may therefore be conceived of as working. Normally the conception of work relationships includes the assumption that the persons so associated will form with each other a division of labor such that each will be assigned a certain responsibility for some share of the work and that this responsibility is organized in such a manner that the several contributions mesh and are coordinated, thus giving rise to the need for coordinators and other managerial officials.

The distinction between personal and group goals must be made in order to avoid a confusion. The laymen in the Weiss and Kahn (1960) study referred to above mentioned *payment* in their definition of work. This does not tell us what they are doing, however, but only why they are doing it. Persons will give all kinds of reasons for associating themselves with others to do work — money, prestige, power, satisfaction in doing a good job, keeping occupied, association with a pleasant group of workers, serving the community. Such statements describe perceptions of motivation (to which we will give attention later), and it *is* true that the group goal must provide for the motivation of workers or else they will not be induced to participate in the organization at all. One cannot, however, simply add up the personal goals and somehow end up with a group goal.

The goal of manufacturing aircraft is a group goal for a factory engaging in such work but it is clearly different from the personal goals which all the members of an aircraft plant bring with them to the situation. The factory does not exist *in order to* pay its workers (although it must), it does not exist *in order to* provide pleasant working companions (though it often helps if it does) — it exists to produce airplanes. The factory does that not because its members like airplanes (they may indeed be afraid to travel in them) but because there is a social demand for airplanes, or because persons in certain positions of authority decide that airplanes shall be manufactured and their authority extends to the ability to create the means whereby persons may be brought in in order to carry out that goal. We note how this distinction between group and personal goals is related to the layman's exclusion of pleasure from the definition of work. From this point of view, we would restate his viewpoint as follows: work is participation in group goal attainment without consideration as to whether that participation is consistent with personal goals at all times. The average person will certainly seek personal goal attainment or gratification at all times but, when working, he must be prepared to do many things whether or not they bring him personal gratification. The things that he must do are those that are called for or required by the group goal, which is not of course to say that many things may be *believed* to be called for by the group goal when they are not in fact needed.

A brief commentary on the nature of group goals should be made. A group goal is "a desired state of affairs" for an organization. (Etzioni, 1964, p. 6.) We further defined it as limited and definite. Such a characterization is necessary because one can impose a goal on anything: courtship may be claimed to have the goal of making love and play may be claimed to have the goal of having fun. When we impose the requirement that the goal is *limited,* we are saying that the activity has an imagined end and that consequently one is in a position to estimate the degree of closeness to goal attainment. In contrast, making love is endless; it is brought to a conclusion only by fatigue or by failing interest. Further, when we insist that the goal must be a *definite* one, we are saying that the goal must be clear and recognized by the participants either at the start or certainly at some point in the work process. When this is the case, relationships must de defined so as to maximize the likelihood of attaining the goal. One says: to get to this goal one person must do this and another person must do that. The work organization therefore is a control body for its members. This is a basis too for the layman's conception of work as compulsive or irksome.

The group goal has a disciplining effect and the participant must agree to submit to this discipline. At the same time, in economic organizations, while other values are present, the major criterion for choice among alternatives and for the allocation of the several tasks is held to be that of efficient attainment of goals. When in doubt as to what one should do or what action one should take, one is expected to decide in favor of the line of action which costs less. This raises the question of how cost is to be measured. In the United States it usually is restricted to the costs sustained by the individual firm in which case a great many costs, such as transportation and education, are simply passed on to the community. In underdeveloped countries, industry itself must pay for such costs.

The degree of control that the organization exerts on the individual varies depending on the type of the organization and the type of the culture. In nontotalitarian countries, the control is of only a segment of the worker's personality — his role as a work specialist. The boss expects of the worker only enough to make his appropriate contribution to the achievement of the objectives of the organization. He does not expect, in addition, to be loved (though he is pleased if he is) and he does not expect abandonment of all loyalties to family, church, friends, and state. By contrast in totalitarian countries (including Western industry when it leaves home and goes to the East Indies or Africa), a much larger portion of the worker's personality is controlled. This occurs because group goals are defined differently.

In our culture the goal is defined in terms of the establishment narrowly conceived — the factory, the office, the army, the university — and refers to a product or a service that the establishment produces or provides. In Communist countries the goal is defined by the government as part of the national plan. The worker therefore is told he is not working for this or that establishment or this or that manager: he is working for the community. The manager, no less than the worker, is the servant of the community which is the ultimate authority. The Communist party in turn conceives of itself as the agent of the community; therefore, the worker must give his all, not just his role as a worker. If other loyalties — family, friends, church — intervene, they must be given up since a loyalty which interferes with a man's loyalty to the community is by definition subversive or treasonable. The worker who slows down on a job hence is not simply lazy; he is guilty of sabotage. By contrast the worker who gives his all and contributes beyond expected minima ("the activist") is rewarded not merely with money and other emoluments, but is made a "Hero of Labor" — a political or a social rather than an economic reward (Bendix, 1956, pp. 417-433). Although the amount of personality control varies in different countries, the group goal nevertheless requires that there be *some* control or definition of behavior and therefore that there exists some authority structure, as well, of course, as a division of labor.

Many might conclude that the authority structure was a consequence of the division of labor. The attempt to carry out large-scale tasks requires, one might reason, that the task be broken up. It then would follow, rationally, that the tasks that were broken up would have to be coordinated and those who coordinate the task would inevitably assume positions of power and authority over those under them. Warner (1949, p. 8) uses such an argument as a basis for the assumption that stratification is inevitable. Udy's (1958) work would suggest that authority *precedes* specialization. From his work on bureaucratic organizations in 19 societies (all nonindustrial), he concluded that the existence of superiors who had rewards to distribute could be found independently of specialization, but not the reverse. It thus may be that there must exist in a society a structure of the differential allocation of rewards before a specialization develops. Perhaps then those in such positions create organizations in which they can administer power (though not necessarily for that reason).

Common sense also suggests that specialization within organizations proceeds according to rational criteria so that tasks are divided up on the basis of technical norms. Such indeed does take place; however in addition to technical there are also moral norms. It is believed, for example, that a job should be assigned on the basis of qualifications but also that specific jobs are appropriate only to people with a certain skin color, a certain ethnic background, or who have been to a certain educational institution. Similarly, clusters of tasks will grow up and be conceived of as jobs when there may be little reason except force of tradition for so conceiving them. The medieval mysteries of barbering, blood-letting, and tooth-drawing thus were carried out by a single person who felt them to be connected intrinsically. The church in medieval times also had a great variety of functions in addition to the saving of souls: the care of the sick and needy, the subsidization of art and education and the economic function of controlling the guilds through the "just price." The present-day church minister must do more than preach and conduct rituals: he should raise money, have tea with the elderly ladies in the neighborhood, and run a boy scout troop. There seems to be no rational explanation for the fact that the high school teacher of science is felt to be the natural choice to be the high school coach. Similarly Thorner (1942) points out that pharmacists are expected not only to prepare medicines but to sell them, a combination of functions which is not always easy to blend, the danger being that involvement in one may threaten the performance of the other.

In the university, ideally the functions of teaching, research, and community service are expected to be combined; however pressures have been arising which have been splitting them apart. The General Education movement produced an emphasis on "good" teaching in its own right, while an increasing number of persons in the physical and social sciences are hired away by industry and the government to do research, or carry on such research within the university, regarding teaching as a secondary and rather onerous duty. Others become specialized in community service, spending much of their time at it as individuals or at branches of the university which concentrate on extension. Work clusters such as these combine and separate over time.

Workshops

Among the many forms of work organization, the most important have been the guild, the putting-out system, and the factory. Guilds reached their climax in the thirteenth century in Europe and have not yet entirely disappeared from the earth. Guilds were of several types, some being mainly religious fraternities, others being concerned with craft and merchant activity. The distinctive feature of the guild that marked it off from other forms of work organizations was that both masters and workers were found together in the same association. The guild grew up partly as a protective association and partly to keep control over the membership and maintain certain standards in manufacturing and distribution. Members attempted to monopolize the available work for there was competition from the monastic orders, rural craftsmen, and independent artisans (Moore, 1951, p. 19). In addition they controlled entry and limited the trade that particular guilds might enjoy. Control went considerably beyond matters of price and standards of work. As Mumford (1938) points out the guilds began as religious fraternities and never entirely lost their religious nature. They enjoyed the patronage of a saint and provided a decent burial for their members. The "brothers ate and drank together on regular occasions; they formulated regulations for the conduct of their craft; they planned and paid for and enacted their parts in the mystery plays, for the edification of their fellow townsmen; and they built chapels, endowed chantries, and founded schools." (Mumford, 1938, pp. 29-30.)

Within the guild, the main positions were those of master, apprentice, and journeyman. The master was not a boss in the modern sense of the term. He owned the shop itself but not the tools that the workmen had. He did not supervise the work but rather was the most skilled of the workmen present; but he was, of course, ulti-

11

mately responsible for the product that the guild turned out. The apprentice enjoyed a close intimate relation with his master, in effect becoming part of the master's family. A journeyman was a person who had completed his apprenticeship but did not own a shop of his own. Indeed as the controls on entry tightened over the years, the journeymen became essentially day laborers. Later certain guilds became dominant over others to the point where certain masters became major political figures in the town. The death blow to the guild system was dealt by the coming of great new markets beyond the seas and the large expansion of population (Schneider, 1957, pp. 35-36). Still later, the coming of modern nations with powerful central governments making possible safe trade over vast areas resulted in independent agents and owners setting up shop anywhere free of guild controls. These new merchants soon outstripped the old guilds.

The putting-out system, (Gay, 1932) which lasted from the fifteenth to the eighteenth centuries in Europe, made use of the large numbers of rural persons who had been uprooted and depressed by population changes and enclosure movements. A merchant with some capital supplied these persons with materials with which they might work in their homes, such as wool to be spun or cloth to be cut. The merchant would appear later and pay for the material in cash. At first workers owned their own tools since such tools were simple. Later the relationship was converted into a straight wage payment for services rendered. Even then the method proved relatively inefficient because of the lack of supervision of production by the merchant. Merchants therefore sought to tie workers more closely to them by renting out more complex tools to them and developing a debt tie between themselves and the workers. Since the work was carried out at home and since the desire for income was high, it became the pattern for the entire family to work. This pattern persisted and was mainly responsible for the child labor practice which was so widespread in the early period for the factory system. It was not the owners of the factories who opposed attempts to abolish child labor but the children's parents who had never known any other arrangement except that of child labor either on the farm or under the putting-out system (Bendix, 1956, pp. 36-37).

The factory form of production has succeeded in pushing out other forms because it is enormously more efficient and far more dependable. It brings workers together in one place and eliminates the expense of transporting raw materials from rural cottage to rural cottage. With workers under the same roof work supervision and enforcement of discipline are easier. Such an efficient form of production was called for by the new nations with their astronomical needs for gunpowder, weapons, uniforms, new roads and means of communications, docks and other forms of transportation and all of the other instruments of a modern state. Stimulating the growth of the factory were new sources of capital from the new world and, of course, the powerful motivation provided by the Calvinistic ethic in which man saw his work as a means of securing a sign of grace.

It was not, however, the factory alone that was distinctive but rather the fact that this form of production was organized in the corporate manner. Although corporations of different kinds have been known at various times in the past, the distinctly modern corporation is a new phenomenon in the world. It was developed apparently by the merchants of the Hanseatic League in order to finance ships, warehouses, and costly forms of transportation and to spread out the risk of loss while the goods were on the high seas (Moore, 1951, pp. 42-43). The distinctive feature of the modern corporation is that it can sue and be sued as an entity quite apart from the individuals who compose the organization. Since a stockholder was not held liable for the debts of the enterprise, he therefore could put as much as he pleased into the company without being responsible beyond this amount for the debts of the company. Through this means it became possible for the first time in history to gather together huge amounts of capital and to enjoy the benefits of large scale.

At the same time the corporate form raises new questions about how the affairs of the company are conducted. Since the owners are widely dispersed and many are banks or financial institutions rather than private persons, it is not at all clear who the effective owners of the corporation are. Such dispersal of ownership means that most of these persons will have little interest in how the corporation is run provided they enjoy what they consider a good return on their investment. One effect is that a relatively small group of investors who may own only a small per cent of the stock may, because they are well organized and of one mind, exercise effective control over the board of directors and hence over the management. In turn management, while supposedly hired employees of the stockholders, will in practice have a relatively free hand in how the corporation is run, subject only to possible removal. Under these circumstances persons who do not own the corporation may in fact control and direct it. Some managers will be more interested in a share of the market than they will in profit and others began to think of themselves as "professional" managers who see their tasks largely as that of assuring the survival of the corporation (Moore, 1962, pp. 14ff). Although the corporation is the dominant form of organization, it is by no means the only one or even the most common as we shall see later.

Work and Identity

To some men their occupation is so important that it is virtually identical with their personalities. Such was the original sense of "vocation" which meant, literally, a "calling." A man felt that he had been called to his work by higher forces which he was serving and consequently had an obligation to try to be especially proficient or dedicated. At the other extreme is the attitude of the worker: his occupation is simply a means whereby he secures money. He is quite likely to change it if something better comes along. Most people who work seem to fall somewhere between these two limits. Bakke (1939) showed that when a group of skilled workers became unemployed, they were not at first willing to accept jobs different from those they usually performed. This was partly a matter of wage differences, but at least as important was the fact that they had developed some identification with their craft and were reluctant to change jobs because this would mean a change in the way these men saw themselves.

Dubin (1956) attempted to assess the importance of the job to industrial workers in three midwestern plants. He found that only 24 per cent of these workers were job-oriented in their life interests. In other words three-quarters of them found their preferred human associations and contacts outside of their places of employ-

ment. The workplace seemed to be relatively unimportant for primary human relationships and did not evoke significant sentiments
and emotions from workers. Orzack (1959) attempted to find out
whether the same thing was true of a group of 150 professional
nurses whom he studied. Professional persons, he speculated, ought
to find their work more significant in their life interests. On the
whole this was the case. Whereas 85 per cent of Dubin's workers
received their important personal satisfaction off the job, only one-
third of Orzack's nurses did. Two-thirds found their prime personal
satisfactions in their work. A significant consideration in such studies is the extent to which the job *permits* a person to find personal
satisfactions at work. Such professions as optometry or dentistry
do not allow a person to find colleagues with whom he can develop
informal ties at work. He thus will be forced to seek personal satisfaction with colleagues outside of the work situation, if he seeks
them at all.

An important area of study has made use of the concept of alienation in work (Arendt, 1958; Bell, 1960, Chapter 16; Pappenheim,
1959). Alienation has been used in various senses — by some to refer
to the effects on the worker of the facts that he does not own the
machine and tools with which he works, that he is an employe on
somebody else's property, and that he makes only a small contribution to the product. Important studies of alienation have been made
by Blauner (1962) who has examined it in a variety of industrial
settings. Blauner conceives of alienation as a process of fragmenta-
tion in which the person sees himself not as a whole human being
but as a "thing" which is being manipulated. Alienation includes
five major dimensions: powerlessness, meaninglessness, normlessness, isolation, and self-estrangement. (Seeman, 1959.) Blauner
examines the extent to which these five dimensions are present in
four different kinds of industry: printing (a craft industry), textiles
(a machine-tending industry), automobile assembly work (an assembly line industry), and the chemical industry (a continuous
process industry). On the dimension of powerlessness, Blauner
finds that printers are not alienated at all. They are able to control
the pace of work, choose the tools they use, control quality and,
partially, the work output itself. On the other hand in textiles control cannot be exercised as easily, since the pace and rhythm of work

15

are set by the way machines are set up and organized. In addition, supervision is close.

Predictably, Blauner found a maximum of powerlessness in the automobile assembly line worker. When one moved to the most completely automated activity of all, however, namely the chemical industry, powerlessness decreased. Here workers monitor the job and are able to work at their own pace as long as no emergency occurs. Blauner did not find that the operators felt that they were the mere pawns of the technology. When Blauner looked at degree of meaninglessness, he found again that printers felt their work to be quite meaningful: after all they work on entire products and are aware at all times of the contribution that the job makes to the whole. There is a greater sense of meaninglessness in the case of the textile worker and most of all in the automobile worker. For the chemical operator, however, the work again becomes meaningful since attention focuses on the process rather than the particular job, with the worker accepting responsibility for a whole section of the operation. When Blauner turned to normlessness and isolation he found striking differences. The degree of feeling of being integrated by a set of norms and a feeling cohesive with other workers definitely decreases as one moves from craft to the assembly line technology but rises again when one reaches the continuous process technology. The differences, though, are not so great on these dimensions, in part because other bases of integration exist. For example in textiles the plant is usually located in a small town in which traditional paternalistic relationships between workers and management tend to produce a strong sense of unity. In the assembly line technology the high degree of unionization and the tightly knit bureaucracy in the factory link the worker with other workers and the organization itself.

On the dimension of self-estrangement, the craft technology allows for a good deal of self-expression and personal growth. In textiles, monotony is a serious problem but not as serious as one might have predicted. The reason, Blauner finds, is that much of the most deadening and dull work has been taken over by women who do not find the work quite so trying as men apparently do. In addition, as already noted, the worker's self-estrangement is reduced by his close ties with the community and his bosses. Assembly line technology is highly self-estranging but in chemicals the curve again reverses itself. There are long periods of routine but these are broken up by periods of frantic activity whenever emergencies or unexpected breakdowns occur. On the whole Blauner's study leads one to conclude that the burden of proof is on him who claims that the modern manual worker has become alienated from his work. Certainly there are striking differences between industries and in kinds of alienations. Work is apparently not as destructive of man's initiative and creativity as some have insisted.

There have been many studies of outside identities that conflict with work identities. Persons may develop loyalties to a cause, to an outside group, to the very organization where they work (rather than to the job itself) and to their clients. Identification with a cause leads a person to take a strong ideological position and consequently makes him into a difficult person to control. This is often true of persons who lead the fight for important new developments in their fields. However original they might be or even if later they are proved correct, at the time they are likely to be attacked as being upstarts, quacks, or worse. This does not mean that occupations in general are opposed to new developments but rather that those who control the occupation prefer to initiate the new developments from within, and according to accepted procedures. The man who goes all out in favor of a cause, and particularly the one who takes his case to the public (as for example Nurse Sister Kenny), is rejecting his colleagues and their opinions. Whatever the merits of his proposed change, the occupation will be upset at the public airing of linens and will not wish the public to determine whether or not a given practice should be adopted. They wish to maintain control themselves.

Other kinds of identifications outside of occupations may include identification with a race, with one's sex as in the case of female employees, and with labor unions. Racial identifications are common when a people succeeds in penetrating a new occupation for the first time. For example, the first Negro personnel man in a factory has to face the questions Who am I? Am I a personnel man first or am I a Negro first? Since he has had to fight hard initially to get into the position, he may feel a strong identification with his colleagues in the department. What should he do, however, if he discovers that all of the "race" questions are automatically referred to him? In addition what should he do if he finds that there is a quota on Negroes on certain jobs? Should he notify action leaders in the community? If he keeps his silence and it is eventually found out that such a quota in fact exists, he will be accused of being a renegade and of forgetting his own people. On the other hand, if he does inform leaders, his colleagues in the personnel department will feel that he is the type of person who cannot be trusted to keep his mouth shut about company secrets.

This also may be the problem faced by a woman personnel worker who discovers that she has been hired to provide "the woman's point of view." She must answer the question of whether she should fight for the rights of women in the plant or whether she should try to identify with her colleagues in the personnel department. Sometimes union leaders who are also workers will come to value their union affiliation more highly than their work affiliation, and the union may provide a few of them with a new world in which to live. Such identification problems may be faced by foremen who are unable to decide whether they are the representatives of their workers *to* management or whether they are the first line of management in relations with the workers (Roethlisberger, 1945; Strauss, 1957; Walker, Guest and Turner, 1956; Whyte and Gardner, 1945; Wray, 1949).

Still another kind of identity conflict is illustrated by the medical profession in a study by Hall (1948). He found some physicians to be "colleague types" and others to be "individualistic types," that is, some were oriented to their colleagues and others to their patients. The first found that they did not have to seek patients aggressively since they were part of a referral system which kept them supplied with patients. On the other hand the second type had to go out and seek their patients on their own and were forced therefore to be more aggressive, a characteristic for which they were often criticized by the colleague type of physicians. It is important, as we shall show later, that incentive systems used in industry be tied to the kind of identities that people have. Whether such systems succeed or fail often depends on the extent to which they successfully motivate the identities that men have with them while they work.

18

Legitimations of the Right to Manage

Disciplined behavior in the service of work goals requires means for assuring predictability of behavior, coordination of effort, and obedience to commands. Such discipline can be secured by the use of coercion and persuasion, but these methods are time-consuming and require very large staffs. Consequently, organizations develop structures which routinize the disciplinary process. The major approach is through the development of a viable authority structure. Authority is conceived of as legitimate power, such legitimacy referring to its being grounded in a set of common values. Legitimate action is action which is justified in terms of its correspondence to a set of values which persons accept. When action is taken, the command of a superior will be obeyed by subordinates because of a generally accepted belief that such a command conforms to the common value-orientation of the group to which it is addressed. Obeying is therefore simply affirming the values themselves. As Blau and Scott (1962, pp. 143-144) point out, when social norms develop which enforce compliance of the orders that are in accord with the group values, the added weight of group approval is given to the entire process. The member of the group to whom the command is addressed will obey the order because the order is felt to be right and because refusal to do so is an attack on the values the group holds dear. In time such potential group disapproval may not have to be invoked. At this point, authority becomes self-enforcing.

The problem, though, is more than structural. Managers of organizations are faced with the task of justifying their right to wield power. Although Burnham's (1941) thesis of ever-increasing managerial power over the total society is fallacious, managers are highly visible and find themselves required to justify such power as they do have, especially since they do not own the business they manage. The problem is serious since, though management is accountable to many interests — stockholders, suppliers of materials, competitors, employees, and the public — the very diversity of these persons means that managers are in fact accountable to none of them. The notion suggested by Berle and Means (1932) that managers are "trustees" has some merit but gives trouble since it is difficult to reconcile the notion of a trustee with the fact of actual

19

control of policy. "If the relationship is one of trust — a fiduciary position in the archaic language of the law — how does it happen that the trustees have their hands in the till?" (Moore, 1962, p. 8.) Managers are not elected by any organization constituency, but are chosen by their administrative superiors, a process which goes on until it reaches a dispersed group of stockholders and other institutions. According to Moore: "Managers are elected neither by constituents nor, in effect, by stockholders. They cannot claim for themselves the rights of property or the biologically inherited 'divine right' of kings to rule. They lack a doctrine of 'apostolic succession' that would preserve a spiritual linkage with the original founder. Their accession to power is more likely to be marked by a cocktail party than by the rich color of the inauguration of a national president (who has an electorate) or a university president (who has various constituencies including, notably, trustees) or of the head of a church (who has his authority from God alone)." (Moore, 1962, pp. 9-10.)

In recent years the great growth of power of labor unions in the United States has produced an ever-closer scrutiny of the actions of managers. Much of the growth of the staff functions in industry can be traced to increased union pressures; as a result management finds it needs data to justify action publicly which it formerly would have thought little about or would have justified in terms of its "judgment." The memory of the great depression of the 1930's and the recurring recessions in recent years have also brought the manager under increasing attack. If he wishes to take credit for the great productivity of the American economy, then he will be held accountable for its failure to provide full employment and for other economic fluctuations. In addition the test of survival of the business concern itself is not sufficient for the authority of the manager to rest unchallenged. If the corporation is a large one the community will have too great a stake in it to permit it to go under even though it may be very badly managed. In the United States, managers will be changed if corporations are felt to be doing badly but the corporation itself will not be abolished. The relative permanency of the organization, in spite of bad management, is most evident in new countries which are attempting to industrialize in a hurry. Business organizations will often be kept in existence because

20

of their importance to national goals irrespective of how they are managed or whether or not they show a profit.

Trends such as these, as well as changes in the structure of industrial organization itself, affect the kinds of justification managers offer for their authority. Bendix (1956, Chapter 7) has shown that the great accomplishment of Western industry (at home, that is) has been to give workers a legitimate place in the social order by making the ideologies of management applicable to them. If the man at the top were there not by virtue of who he was but of what he had done, and if his accomplishments were a reflection of teachable skills, then others might hope to rise by emulating him. A powerful dynamic and motivation for a bureaucratic orientation thus was provided.

In contrast, in eighteenth and nineteenth century Russia and present-day East Germany, the experience has been different. The Tsars held a monopoly of authority over both managers (whether aristocracy, middle-class entrepreneurs, or state officials) and employees (whether serfs, professional workers, or freemen). The authority of managers was subject to the Tsar's pleasure and employees were therefore to regard the Tsar and not the manager as the ultimate authority. Consequently, their subordination was justified by their political subservience to the Tsar, who was symbolic of the people themselves. In East Germany, the imposition on industry of a double bureaucracy (one line representing state industrial planning, the other representing the SED [Communist] party) leads to a justification of subordination by an insistence that, since the party represents the worker's interest, the worker is subordinate to no manager (for the latter is also subject to the party) but to the community. The worker should give all, therefore, not because he hopes to be a manager some day, but because the community (namely, himself) needs his best efforts. From this point of view, persons will secure the right to manage others if they are felt to be politically loyal or if their values are felt to be consistent with party goals. The good manager is one who is able to fulfill his quota under the national plan, even though, as Berliner (1957) tells us, *Blat* (finagling) may be necessary.

An important shift in the ideologies justifying managerial authority has also taken place over time. Before the 1890's success was justified as a reward for virtue. The increasing bureaucratization of business led to a shift from the idealization of the hero-industrialist to the praise of the organization itself and the opportunities it provided. (Bendix, 1959.) In place of qualities of ruthlessness and competitive drive, one finds idealized the qualities of being able to engineer cooperation and coordinate the vast bureaucracy. A real ambivalence, however, remains. When management repeats that the organization is "one big happy family," Bendix feels the phrase really applies only to management itself and is, hence, a way of increasing its solidarity *vis-à-vis* the lower employees and labor unions. Such a rationale is, then, essentially negative. "The fact is that in this era of bureaucratization the industrialist does not have a fighting creed." (Bendix, 1954, p. 175.)

Kerr, Dunlop, Harbison, and Myers (1960) in a study of industrialism in new countries, suggest that such fighting creeds are particularly important when new industrializing elites attempt to move a country rapidly along the road toward industrialization. They describe the ideologies of five different types of elites. *Dynastic* elites base their authority on the concept that certain families are "called" to manage. *Middle-class* elites rest the authority of managers on the functions they perform, with the right to access to the ranks of management being based on individual initiative and competence. *Revolutionary intellectuals* as industrializing elites justify the role of managers as servants of the party and the state. *Colonial administrators* rationalize managerial authority in terms of the superiority of the nationals of the home country the managers represent. Last, *nationalist* leaders conceive of managerial resources as an obviously necessary instrument for industrial development which in turn contributes to national development. Kerr, *et al.* (1960) conclude that the role of management is no longer on the defensive but is accepted as indispensable for industrialization. Indeed, it is increasingly recognized that it is easier to train a whole work force in minimal industrial skills than to recruit and train a set of committed industrial managers.

The Moral Structure of Work Relationships

Those who view work as little more than a bargain or contract between an employer and an employee see the employee as offering a skill or some other capability to his employer. Such a skill is a part of the man's personality which he is "selling." Furthermore this skill represents the limit of what he is expected to contribute. Nevertheless the individual cannot himself take only a part of his personality with him to the work situation. When he asks for a promotion he therefore is likely to offer as a justification not only job related factors but also family or other personal needs. Furthermore his employer does not behave quite as rationally as it is often claimed that he does. Persons will be chosen for their jobs on the basis of competence but in addition race, religion, sex and other personal criteria, which have come to be attached to the job al-‘ though having little to do with its successful performance, will also be taken into account. Malinowski called our attention to the fact that when a Trobriand Islander was building a canoe for a long ocean trip, *two* things were done to the canoe so that it would not sink: the canoe was properly shaped *and* magic was performed over it. When we study work scientifically, we expect of course that each job will have certain technical qualifications but we shall also be alert for the *moral* qualifications that will be present.

Industry presents the surprising circumstance that it respects the conceptions of right and wrong held by its customers or employees and may even impose some special ideas of its own. Still the logic of industrialization often forces industry to reduce discriminatory practices. After all if a firm is to be successful it must have a competent labor force. This may mean that it is compelled to hire persons whose race, sex, or personal beliefs may go contrary to the views of management or of community. As a consequence it is industry that has been one of the great agents of social change throughout the world, breaking up castes in India and affecting the nature of race relations in the United States and elsewhere. This does not mean, however, that the moral structure of work has vanished. It means only that it has changed.

A striking example of the moral structure of work is provided by the sex-typing of occupations. It is, of course, widely known that the proportion of women working is increasing and that this has been accompanied by women's invasion of many previously male occupations. This does not mean, however, that the tendency of certain jobs to be men's jobs and others to be women's has vanished, for when women invade a previously male occupation the effect is usually to make these jobs into women's jobs. When women move into an area, in other words, they take it over from the men. Some twenty occupations account for almost three-quarters of all employed women; more than one-half are found in only eight occupations. (National Manpower Counsel, 1957, pp. 58ff.) These occupations tend strongly to be women's occupations: nearly one-half of all working women are found in an occupation in which three-quarters or more of the members of the occupation are women. The amount of sexual segregation in occupations goes even further than these statistics suggest. For example though three-quarters of all teachers are women, that figure fails to suggest the true degree of sexual segregation in teaching. The small proportion of men tend to be concentrated in high schools and in certain subjects such as the physical sciences and some of the social sciences, which tend overwhelmingly to be taught by men.

Another type of pattern suggesting the moral structure of work is shown by examining the way in which occupations are stratified with reference to one another, often in strange ways. In the ministry or priesthood, one finds "church-builders," "clean-up men" (clergymen who specialize in helping settle the debts of a church that has gotten into difficulty with its creditors), "peace-men" (persons sent to mediate disputes) and "funeral preachers." In university departments, in addition to specialties about which everyone knows, there will be also informal specialties. Some men thus will be known as scholars, others as good administrators, some as outstanding teachers and others as highly skilled in securing research funds. Men will form opinions of one another in terms of *these* specialties as well as the specialties that their clients (their students) know about. From these specialties it is but a step to specialties which are essentially expressions of segregation by race, sex or religion or any other category that society considers important.

For example to say that Negro physicians treat Negro patients and white physicians treat white patients does not actually describe the facts. In general, white physicians have a monopoly of the treatment of both whites and Negroes (Williams, 1946) but that fact does not exhaust the picture of the division of labor. The trade that Negro physicians enjoy includes the cases which white physicians do not wish to handle, such as cases of whites' suffering from venereal or other shameful diseases which the white physician will refer to the Negro. Another type of division of labor is observed in studies of the Negro lawyer, as Hughes and Hughes (1952, pp. 96-97) describe it:

> *To the poor Negro, the law is trouble to be got out of. A lower class Negro wants to win an insurance case against a utility or an employer, a Negro woman has a son in jail and wants to get him out. They often believe that a white lawyer can manipulate all these institutions better than a Negro lawyer could: it is, after all, a white man's world. . .on the other hand a middle-class Negro wants a divorce which has already been agreed upon; he wants a deed, articles of partnership or incorporation or advice regarding a contract. It is "friendly" law. He goes to the Negro lawyer and feels very loyal to his race.*

Similarly the middle classes of many ethnic and racial minorities have attained success by catering to the needs of their own people, whether those are for special newspapers in their language, special clothing, special food or special religious needs. Whatever the truth, this group lays itself open to the charge of having a stake in continuing segregation. Where, it is asked, would the editor of a Negro newspaper be able to earn a living if segregation did not make people willing to buy a newspaper which concentrated on describing racial incidents? It is easy to exaggerate this point, particularly since editors may be in the forefront in the fight against segregation. Still, there is no denying the fact that race differences have provided a special place for such editors in the division of labor. Instances such as these support the claim that in addition to a technical division of labor there is also a moral division of labor in every society.

CHAPTER 2

INDUSTRY AND THE COMMUNITY

THE effects of work spread out beyond the individual to family, community, government and society. An organization will not even be permitted to exist unless it is regarded as legitimate by both society and the state. In addition an industry cannot continue for long if it takes no account of the social expectations of its labor force and the kinds of work conditions they consider proper. Such problems have been solved in the industrialized countries, but they come up repeatedly in the newer nations as well as in the older ones from time to time. In particular, we are facing a whole new set of social changes incidental to the automation of industry. These considerations make it clear that industry cannot be understood in isolation from its social environment.

Legitimation of the Right to Produce and Serve

The goals of an organization are seen as goals only by those inside the organization. To outsiders, they are means or facilities. Thus the goal of a firm may be the production of shoes but obviously shoes are a means that the customer uses to enable him to go about his everyday affairs properly dressed. Viewed in this way, finding out what the goal of an industry is is essentially a matter of "determining a relationsip of the organization to the larger society, which in turn becomes a question of what the society (or elements within it) want done or can be persuaded to support." (Thompson & McEwen, 1958, p. 23.)

If the goal of an organization, then, is the way in which it relates itself to the surrounding society the study of goals becomes an inquiry into the ways in which organizations are legitimated—that is, accepted as proper by others in the society. In the case of business organizations legitimation is secured directly by the ability to make a profit and hence stay in business. With that criterion, the particular product or service produced (it might even be harmful) is secondary. The ability to make a profit or supply a desired product is, however, not in itself enough. Even to make a profit business organizations must pay attention at least to public attitudes to the company or to the products, if only to avoid governmental controls.

The phrases "robber-baron" and "money-changer" often were used by some early writers on business but it is not at all clear whether or not they presented an accurate picture. The evidence seems to be that it was greatly overdrawn. Jones (1953) finds that in present-day literature the businessman is not depicted as evil but as frustrated and unhappy. On the whole the results of the many polls dealing with attitudes towards businessmen have tended to bear out this picture. Such attitudes have been rather favorable. For example, during the Great Depression of the 1930's, a poll (conducted in 1937) reported that 75 per cent of persons with an opinion felt that big business concerns were good for the country (Cantril and Strunk, 1951, p. 335). A more recent study (Survey Research Center, 1951) came to a similar conclusion. Some 76 per cent of the population said that they believed the advantageous effects of business outweighed the disadvantageous effects. Furthermore they did not believe that big business was more powerful than small business, labor or the state and national government. They felt further that big business paid better wages than small business and provided more job security for the employee. There is some feeling that prices are not set competitively (Hickman and Kuhn, 1956, pp. 118-119). In general, findings from studies such as these suggest that business occupies a well-established place in American society although persons are not unwilling to criticize the conduct of business affairs.

Another kind of legitimation takes place through the ties that business organizations establish with one another. One firm thus may be the supplier of raw materials for another firm, may finance its operations or have other types of relationships with it. Some of these may be extremely complex, depending on the kind of bargaining that goes on within the firm. In addition, firms may be related through multiple ownership as in the case of overlapping memberships in boards of directors. A study by Goldner (1960) of labor relations representatives in organizations unearthed a novel type of relationship between organizations. Goldner found that these representatives played what he called "boundary roles." Since they spent so much of their time negotiating with labor unions they came to be viewed by their own management as being somewhat union-oriented. At the same time unions were uneasy about them, feeling that they knew more than was comfortable about the way in which the union ran its affairs. These persons thus played marginal positions, operating on the boundary between the company and the union. Their very marginal positions were used by the men in doing their jobs better. They were able to carry trial balloons back and forth from management to the union and vice versa without committing either management or the union.

Relationships between organizations have not been sufficiently studied (Litwak and Hylton, 1962). Although one would expect that relationships among business organizations would be determined wholly by commercial advantage, in time, firms develop ties with one another which are controlled by norms and values other than those that are limited strictly to business. After all those who run business firms desire predictability of supplies and dependability, and it is always possible to use friendship and the ties of tradition to secure more favorable terms than one could obtain simply by bargaining. Thus will develop what Durkheim long ago called noncontractual elements in contracts, a phenomenon studied recently by Macaulay (1963).

Major Industrial Trends

We shall consider first the long range trends then turn to developments in the last decade, some of which represent important shifts in these trends. Over the last half century clerical and professional workers have increased strikingly in absolute and relative terms. Semiskilled workers did likewise until recently, actually declining proportionately in the last decade. Skilled workers have increased more slowly. Proprietors, managers and officials have barely managed to retain the same proportion of the working force and unskilled workers have actually been declining both absolutely and relatively. (Fichlander, 1955; Gross, 1958, Chapter 3.)

The great increase in clerical workers has been due to the increase in the importance of administrative activity in business (including such activities as accounting, promotions and sales) and the increase in the number and complexity of governmental services. Clerical workers now make up nearly one-fourth of the working force but they are not an influential group nor a powerful one. There is little control on their entry so it is difficult to train them in any set of ethical or social controls as the professions and those industries that are highly unionized train their entrants. In addition they are poorly organized because of remaining hopes of upward mobility and because of their closeness to management. Attempts to organize the white-collar workers have not so far been encouraging although in some places a high proportion may be unionized, providing unionization in the whole community is general. The city of Seattle affords such an example.

A second reason for the lack of organized power of clerical workers stems from the fact that females make up some 60 per cent of all white collar workers. It remains true that women workers occupy an ambiguous position in the labor force. Children may interfere with a woman's ability to continue working and, in any case, in our society the wife is not expected to be the sole provider but rather to supplement the family income. Consequently she does not usually identify with her job to the same extent that her husband does.

Trends, however, are dynamic. Labor-saving devices make it increasingly possible for housework to be done in less and less time. Families remain relatively small, and women make additional use of facilities for looking after their children while they work. For a larger and larger number of married women, jobs are permanent and are taken seriously (Nye and Hoffman, 1963, Chapters 1-3).

The great increase in professional workers is due to the increase in the number of persons in the traditional profession and to the emergence of new professions in such areas as public health, teaching, engineering, social work, and accounting. The largest increase has been in the technological professions such as engineering, chemistry, designing and drafting. Among proprietors, managers and officials, disparate groups are included. Farmers, one of the main components of this category, have been decreasing in numbers and as a proportion of the labor force. A second reason for the slow growth of the category of proprietors, managers and officials has been the lack of growth of self-employment. Owners of many small businesses, forced out, had to go to work in someone else's firm. Helping to keep up numbers in this category, though, are middle management executives and other organization men who have increased along with large-scale organization.

The great changes in the make-up of the manual work force are related to work mechanization. Skilled workers have found their skills being taken over by machines, making them semiskilled workers or unemployed persons, although the increase in population and demand has prevented this group from declining and indeed has enabled it to increase its proportion of the working force moderately. The unskilled workers are, however, declining in actual numbers. One effect of these trends has been a change in the "craft." Companies no longer look for tailors or mechanics but for sewing machine operators and punch press operators. As a consequence workers have become increasingly organized not in terms of craft but in terms of industry or machines or process. Labor unions such as the "United Automobile Workers" will include many who have nothing at all to do with making automobiles and the Teamsters include clerks and salesmen. This trend gives an entirely new dimension to social organization. The former interest in beauty or fine workmanship, now taken over by the machine, is replaced by an interest in uniformity and in the continued operation of the machine.

As skills are transferred to the machine, the designing of these machines becomes highly complex and is lifted up into the professional category, producing the need for the designer and the engineer. The increased use of machines, however, robs work of much of its meaning, makes it boring, and hence creates a need for yet another professional—namely, the personnel man.

As crafts decline and work becomes uniform, few jobs yield much pride in workmanship. It is being discovered, however, that subdividing the job into ever finer parts may not necessarily be the most efficient way of carrying it out (Friedmann, 1961). As a consequence some firms are deliberately enlarging jobs, which has resulted in increased efficiency and work satisfaction. It is also just such finely divided jobs that are most likely to be automated and hence to disappear altogether as specialties.

Trends in the last decade are well summarized in the Manpower Reports of the President (1963 and 1964). There have been two major recent changes. First the shift from goods-producing to service-producing industry has accelerated since 1957. The proportion of all workers in the goods-producing industry (agriculture, mining, manufacturing and construction) dropped from 51 per cent in 1947 to 42 per cent in 1962. On the other hand growth has continued in the service industries (transportation and public utilities; trade; finance, insurance, and real estate; service and miscellaneous industry; and government). The government is one of the most rapidly growing of the service industries. Numbers employed rose from 5.5 million in 1947 to 9.2 million in 1962, or more than two-and-a-half times as fast as all nonfarm employment. Contrary, though, to the beliefs of some, this growth has not been at the national level but rather at the state and local level where approximately three-fourths of all government workers are found. Such growth has been primarily in hospitals, sanitation services and, in particular, in education.

Farm employment continues its long range drop from some 50 per cent of the labor force in 1870 to about 7 per cent at present. The over-all trend for manufacturing is less easy to describe. Manufacturing registered gains until it reached a peak in 1920 when it made up approximately 30 per cent of the working force. It has not been able to increase its proportion appreciably above that since. In 1962 the number in manufacturing was 16.8 million, representing about 23 per cent of the labor force (27.7 per cent of employed persons). The fact that a constant or even a declining per cent of the labor force has been able to provide all of the needs for manufactured goods for the rapidly increasing population is, of course, testimony to the great increase in productivity of manufacturing. At the same time the fact that it has been unable to exceed its 1920 proportion of the employed suggests that it has been able to maintain its position as the largest single industry division not because of the population increase but because of the continued increase in demand for manufactured goods.

The second major shift has been the much faster growth of white-collar occupations over blue-collar occupations in the general economy. In 1956, for the first time in history, professional and managerial, clerical and sales employees outnumbered employees in manual occupations. In fact, the increase in white-collar workers accounted for most of the increase in *all* fields of work in the period since 1947.

The data on trends in size of business organizations present several puzzles and surprises. Woytinsky (1953, p. 342) estimates that no more than one-seventh of farmers and one-half of non-agriculture employers hire as much as a single man-year of labor during a whole year. The following data enable us to assess the distribution of firms by size.

Table 1

Employer Firms Reporting to Old Age and Survivors Insurance, and Their Employees, by Size of Firm, January-March 1953 (in per cent)

Size of Firm (number of employees)		Employers (firms)	Employees
0-	3	59.8	6.9
4-	7	20.4	7.4
8-	19	12.1	10.2
20-	99	6.4	17.7
100-	999	1.2	21.1
1,000-	9,999	0.1	18.6
10,000-	Or more	.01	18.0
Total		100.00	100.0

Source: Data provided by the Bureau of Old Age and Survivors Insurance in Charles B. Spaulding, Introduction to Industrial Sociology. Chandler: San Francisco, 1962.

From this table a striking fact emerges. On the one hand it is clear that the United States is a nation of small firms, for some 90 per cent of firms employ fewer than 20 workers; those employing over 100 make up just a trifle over one per cent. This 90 per cent group of firms all together accounts for less than one-quarter of all employees, whereas the tiny group of large firms (employing over 100) together employ close to 60 per cent of all workers. Firms thus *are* small but, on the average, most employees work for large firms. Data provided by McKean (1958) do not, however, support the common assertion that small business is declining in the United States. He finds that over the last half century small business units have made up from 84 to 90 per cent of all businesses. Other data on the assets, income, and earnings of small business support his conclusion that small business demonstrates a continuing ability to persist in spite of the inroads of large scale organization.

The Family

Traditional research suggested a lack of compatibility between the large, extended family and modern industrialism. The initial effect of industrialism was to separate the farm family from the land and break up the patterns of integration represented by rural living. Roles within the family became differentiated as the man took over breadwinning functions exclusively, with the wife concerning herself more and more with the role of housewife. Later, with the change of attitudes toward child labor, children were defined as incompetent minors. The result was to make the family completely dependent upon the economic work of the father. At the same time, the status of the family became substantially equivalent to the status of the father. A child might rise up or fall below his father's social class but only by leaving the family and operating alone or forming a family of his own. The tendency for large families to live under the same roof became less common in part because of mobility and in part because of the high cost of land in the city. As traditional ties of property and extended family obligations declined, the stability of the family came increasingly to depend on harmonious relationships between husband and wife, a fact which in turn led to much greater emphasis on the independence of the young and on the romantic complex in mate selection.

Recent research has begun to cast doubt on the extent to which the foregoing picture is an accurate reflection of trends. Axelrod

(1956), Young and Willmott (1957), and Aldous (1962) have suggested that the pattern in which members of the same extended family lend things to one another, visit with one another, and help one another in common problems is still of importance in the family even in the modern industrial city. Abegglen (1958) and Johnson (1960) have shown how the extended family may be quite compatible with industrialization in the case of modern Japan. In addition, many writers have noted the manner in which the family has been used traditionally to make large amounts of investment capital freely available to the family members. Indeed, before the coming of the modern corporation and limited liability, the extended family provided the only important means for bringing together large amounts of capital for investment purposes. Studies of migratory laborers show how entire families including extended kin may migrate together, developing a technology and appropriate set of motives and ideologies for such movement. A detailed picture is presented by Davis (1946) for the case of lower class families. A member of a large lower class family assumes that his kin will assist him should he require help and he in turn expects to give aid to his relatives should he have a good job. Through this means the family is able to survive as a large unit when it could not survive at all if it were broken up into a set of small nuclear families.

Since the father is away from home, some commentators on the family have claimed that he can no longer serve as a role model for his sons since the work that he does may be unknown to the son, invisible, or too complex to explain. There is certainly some basis for this claim, yet a high proportion of occupations such as those in construction and others carried out in the open are not difficult to understand or appreciate. Even for those cases where the occupation is complex or esoteric, the father may serve as important a function as ever. Faris (1947) offers the thought that the most important thing a father can transmit is a set of drives and ambitions or a set of points of view, and this is surely just as likely to occur whether the son understands what the father does for a living or not.

In the United States, approximately one-third of married women are working, a figure that approaches one-half for married women in the older years especially in their thirties and forties. Although the tendency is not as strong as it once was, it is still true that the lower the economic level of the husband, the more likely his wife is to be working. Schneider (1957, pp. 441-442) shows how the motives for working vary by social class. In the upper classes a woman may work to keep from being bored, to express herself, or to satisfy her interests. Further down the class scale, the motives are likely to be more strongly economic. At the same time the woman's ability to hang on to her job is harder since she cannot call upon domestic help as readily as the upper class woman.

A much neglected study is that of employed children. Contrary to popular beliefs, child labor has not vanished even in the United States. The percentage of those officially known to be employed between the ages of 10 and 15 is approximately 6 per cent for boys and 3 per cent for girls, a high proportion of whom are found on farms. These figures unquestionably understate the case, since facts on childhood employment are likely to be concealed. Indeed since the middle class family emphasizes the importance of positive attitudes towards business and salesmanship, it would be surprising if these families did not provide a setting in which youngsters felt strongly encouraged to enter the labor market at quite tender ages in some capacity or other.

An early specialization occurs among those who leave school at an early age. The largest group of males between the ages of 14 and 19 is found among operatives and kindred workers, while the largest proportion of girls is found among clerical and kindred workers. It is tragic that these are the very jobs with the poorest future since they are subject to technological displacement. At the other end of the age scale, the role of the aged in industrial society has become a subject of research in its own right. Although the proportion of the population over 65 has been increasing, it is not true that there has been a corresponding increase among older working persons; just the reverse has occurred. The average working life of white male workers is now approximately what it was fifty years ago (around 41 years) while in the meantime the period spent in retirement has been increased from 9.5 years to 15.9 years. Over the last half century, the proportion of older males working has been steadily declining, but female employment participation among the elderly has remained steady. The elderly are not evenly distributed by occupations. Among males, older persons make up 6.5

per cent of managers, officials, and proprietors except farm but only 2.7 per cent of operatives and kindred workers. The higher percentages in the higher ranking occupations may reflect a greater life expectancy among those persons but it is more likely, as Schneider (1957, p. 450) suggests, a reflection of the greater ability of higher status men to decide the age of their retirement themselves. The positive evaluation of work creates problems for the retired, and their attitude to work may affect their subsequent adjustment (Loether, 1964).

Government and the Wider Community

Traditional work patterns in a community can be articulated with industrial needs. Arensberg (1942) has shown how many plastics manufacturing plants in New England were enabled to persist, in spite of their inability to pay competitive wages, by the fact that the local population was accustomed to shift to farming when the demand of the factories for labor fell off seasonally and at other times. Another important relationship between industry and the community revolves about the location of industry. The most important needs from industry's point of view are an adequate source of power and cheap raw materials. Where these happen to be found together industry will often be located, as in the case of the many towns built on mining deposits. Such towns may or may not survive, depending on the value and extent of the resources. Some will disappear, but a few like Kimberly, South Africa, based on diamonds and Sudbury, Canada, based on nickel, have maintained their size. In addition industry usually will attempt to select a location near a good supply of labor, a market and a source of capital. These factors ordinarily mean locating in or near a city.

In cities, manufacturing firms are usually found near the center or in industrial suburbs. Light manufacturing is usually found near the center, with heavy manufacturing relegated to the suburbs because of its need for large amounts of space. Light manufacturing can locate on the second and third floors of older buildings in which one also finds wholesaling, storage, and other activities. Suburban location may be preferred not only because of lower costs of land but because of the ability of firms to band together and reduce costs for common facilities such as parking space, power lines, and the disposal of waste products. In addition a united front can be presented to the complaints of residents of the area against the smoke and other noxious accompaniments of industrial production. Once a considerable group of firms locates in one place, it becomes worthwhile for railroads and other major transporters to build spur lines and freight sheds in the suburbs so that the disadvantage of being away from the freight depots of the railroads in the downtown area is reduced. The very fact of existence of such industrial suburbs points to the need for care in viewing all suburbs as being composed of middle management people on their way up, an impression that might be left by reading a work such as W. H. Whyte's (1956). Some suburbs may be composed largely of working class persons as shown in the works of Berger (1960) and Dobriner (1958, 1963).

One-industry towns, though becoming less common, are still of interest from a sociological viewpoint. Their most striking feature is the tension and resentment between the industry and the town. Members of the community often resent and may even deny the importance of the industry to the town. At the same time the owners or members of management are likely to feel that the population is not sufficiently grateful for the benefit the industry represents. In some communities managements have tried to emphasize the importance of the firm by paying off workers in silver dollars. As these flood through the community, it is thought that merchants and businessmen will realize how dependent they are on the industry. Such a device is likely to produce only a sense of moral outrage and hence to boomerang.

When industry was small, local customs regulated industrial affairs. Business might dominate the community not because it desired to do so or felt that it should do so but rather because there was no other power available to counterbalance business control. The great growth of industry in the latter half of the nineteenth century and the coming of international markets quickly led to a breakdown of these local controls. Government became important as the only institution capable of controlling industry in the interests of the community. For example, hazards to health resulting from smoke and the dumping of industrial waste were regulated and other laws were enacted governing working conditions. It was not entirely a matter of regulation. As industry expanded it desired and even required services from the government such as gas, sewage disposal, employment bureaus, educational facilities, and transportation networks. Still later the government's role was evident in workmen's compensation and wage and hour laws, the control of labor-management relations, vehicle licensing and interstate commerce, monopoly, and international trade.

Form and Miller (1960, p. 147) point out that many government regulations cannot be regarded as interference with business since many of them are the direct result of industry's specific wishes. Examples are laws dealing with free trade, limiting monopoly, providing tariff protections against foreign competition, and limiting union power. Form and Miller (1960, p. 147) further claim that business usually will be forced to take an interest in politics since it surely will wish governmental services to continue, will want the cost of those services kept down, will desire a government sympathetic to it and one willing to limit the power of organized labor, and, finally, will be interested in government because government is a major consumer of goods and services. As a consequence, industries have formed various political organizations, such as the National Steel Institute, the National Association of Manufacturers, and the Association of the American Railroads, in order to pursue their own interests. At the same time, organized labor has also been interested in politics. At first it attempted to create a definite labor party and to father other types of radical parties. Since the time of Samuel Gompers, labor has in general avoided support of any third party but this does not mean that it is no longer interested in politics. The Political Action Committee of the Congress of Industrial Organization, Labor's League for Political Education of the American Federation of Labor (LLPE), and the Committee on Political Education (C.O.P.E.) of the AFL-CIO testify to labor's continuing interest and involvement in politics.

Form and Miller (1960, p. 152) point out two sometimes contradictory roles that the government may play in industrial relations. On the one hand the government acts as the representative of the public interest, occasionally intervening in industrial disputes to prevent a breakdown in the flow of essential goods and services. On the other hand, the government is not always so neutral. It can and does support one side or the other. It may also directly help one side or the other by its power to purchase or refuse to purchase goods and services from various segments of industry. The government cannot be regarded solely as a neutral party in union-management relations.

The Social Structure of Labor Markets

Payment in kind is relatively rare in Western society and not likely to be the whole of a person's remuneration. In periods of economic depression government doles or the benefits distributed by private clinics or social work agencies often take the form of goods or services. Reid (1951) has emphasized the importance of taking into account the value of the housewife's household activities in any discussion of income. Although not "gainful," services are being provided to which a monetary value can be attached and which would have to be purchased in the case of the death of the wife. It is also important to be able to place an economic value on such services so that cross-cultural or trend studies may take account of the great variation in the economic role of the wife. An estimate for 1929 put the dollar equivalent of housewife services at $23 billion (over one-fourth of the national income), and Reid herself valued them at $15 and $34 billion in 1940 and 1945 (about one-fifth of the national income). Payment in kind is more important in some occupations than in others. Household workers receive their employers' cast-off clothes, restaurant workers receive meals, and presidents of universities and nations usually are given the use of a house and the services of a staff. Of all industries, those in farming appear to pay out the largest proportion of their income in kind. One survey estimated the dollar value of non-money income to work out to about 7 per cent of total income for urban families, 17 per cent for rural nonfarm families, and 46 per cent for farm families (Reid, 1951).

Payments in money exhibit important variations which have social significance. Whether income takes the form of wages, fees, salaries, rents, insurance, interest, commissions, bonuses, profit-sharing, dividends, profits, market gambling receipts, or inherited wealth makes an important difference in the prestige which is attached to the income itself. In industry, the distinction between hourly-rated and salaried workers reflects prestige and power differences. If a worker is paid by the hour, it is felt that his labor is a commodity which can be precisely measured in time units of work. The salaried worker's output is thought of as an intangible thing which cannot be measured accurately. He deals with new problems, anticipates future events, and makes complex decisions. One therefore cannot say that two hours of his time is worth exactly twice what one hour is worth. In piecework we encounter a precise relationship between output and income, but this form of payment must be evaluated in terms of theories of motivation to be discussed following.

Although it easily can be exaggerated, the great significance of money in our culture leads wages to become a focus about which many other problems converge. Discussions of wages therefore often mask their concern with other problems. Gouldner's analysis of the factors responsible for a wildcat strike in a gypsum plant calls attention to this problem (Gouldner, 1954, p. 29). An "indulgency pattern," which permitted the men to vary from or even break rules without being punished, had been built up. An injured worker might be permitted (contrary to plant rules) to work in the "sample room" (where the work was light) until he had recovered sufficiently to return to his old job, or workers were allowed to use company equipment for personal use. A new plant administration violated these understandings. The immediate response of the workers was to have their union leaders institute a demand for a 30-cent an hour wage increase. The explanation, Gouldner claims, is that management was within its contractual rights in violating the indulgency pattern and therefore no formal action could be taken against them. The workers turned instead to wages — a contractual issue — and began applying pressure there.

Social scientists have tended to downgrade the importance of size of income as a social factor. Merton (1942) pointed out that although it was true that the members of Warner's upper-upper class were distinguished from the lower-upper class by the fact that the upper-upper class inherited their money, the upper-uppers had to have held on to a great deal of that money or could hardly have manitained their position for long. A study by Miller (1955) of income distribution provides important insights into the significance of amount of income. As is well known, the income curve is badly skewed with a preponderance of cases at the lower end. A considerable part of the skewing is accounted for by the fact that women workers are included and women workers in general make less money than men, even for comparable jobs. When the females are removed from the curve, the curve is still asymmetrical but by no means so extremely. A part of the remaining skewness is attributable to the fact that the unemployed are also included with the employed. If they are removed, a curve results that is still not normal but nevertheless far closer to normal. The remaining bulge at the left in this curve is due to two groups, namely farmers and farm managers (who make up 9 per cent of all workers) and service workers and laborers (17 per cent). The remaining three-quarters of employed men form a highly symmetrical curve, though it is peaked and still contains a tail running out to the high income end of the distribution. Farmers and farm managers present a population with special problems since, unlike urban persons, they can remain in business even when profits become negative. On the other hand, service workers and laborers include the greatest proportion of part-year and other seasonal workers.

In sum, there appear to be a number of separate universes within the population of income recipients and a large part of the skewness of the income curve is removed when these universes are considered separately. The universes result from sex differentiation of work roles, part-time work, part-year work, and ability to stay in business even when income drops very low. Another factor to weight in estimating significance of size of income is hidden expenses. In some occupations the worker must buy his own tools. The physician does not own his own tools, a phenomenon which increases his dependence on the hospital. The scholar has never owned all of his tools — books and journals — although the attempt to own a portion of them helps keep him poor. The engineer has never owned all of his tools either — the machines. Some occupations require

41

special clothing or special expenses which the person must take care of himself and for which he may not be completely reimbursed.

Economic factors accounting for wage structures have included subsistence, wage fund, surplus value, marginal productivity, and bargaining. Social factors are also important. Attempting to describe wages in terms of "importance to society" gets one into difficulty because of the difficulties of defining importance: One could spend a fruitless hour discussing the relative importance of teaching the young and burying the dead without explaining why the latter yields more income than the former. Like any person in it, society will pay as little for an activity as possible and therefore the reward for an activity depends in part, at least, on what society can be required to pay, a fact which frequently makes occupational pay a power phenomenon. Such power manifests itself in various ways. A service in high demand places those who supply it in a position to demand high pay. If the service is in addition of an emergency character, then those who supply it (doctors, lawyers, plumbers, TV repairmen, drug smugglers) can demand more money than those who supply services that can be postponed (architects, librarians, many types of researchers, gardeners, rug shampooers, pimps).

Assuming moderate to high demand, the power of the practitioner to control his income depends further on the rarity of the service and on his market position. A service can remain rare if it involves a natural scarcity, a long period of education and experience, or if those who provide it are organized to control entry to the occupation. Professional and craft services tend to meet these requirements and they help explain their relatively high pay. A professor of dentistry can, however, demand more money than a professor of English not only because the demand for dentistry is higher, but also because the professor of dentistry is in a better market position: He can *withdraw* his services and go into private practice. Similarly, those who are in a position to charge per service or per person (doctors, dentists, lawyers, private investigators, plumbers) can earn more than those who cannot do so (nurses, social workers, teachers, police detectives, maintenance men). Their poor market position helps explain the low wages paid to casual laborers (who, when *seeking* work, must take what they can get) to semiskilled manual workers (who include women, high school students, *etc.*) to policemen, firemen, and soldiers (who though rendering vital and emergency services, are forbidden the right to withhold their services). On the other hand, a good market position is enjoyed by those who are parts of large unions or in industries in which a union settlement with one firm is forthwith adopted in other firms. In addition strong indeed is the market position of the professional in private practice whose services are in high demand; he can take whatever the traffic will bear (which includes the risk of occasionally getting nothing).

The particular character of the labor market is also important. Caplow (1954, p. 151) points out that bureaucracies are often able to offer less money for new recruits because they can offer the recruit tenure or a predictable career. Caplow (1954, pp. 157-177) goes on to describe the structure of the market for semiskilled manual labor, the craftsmen market, the market for professional services, the market for common labor, and such markets as those for unique services, middlemen services, domestic services, and the market for farm hands. Caplow and McGee (1958) point to the difficulty of securing accurate data on the wages which a person who leaves one university to accept a job at another will, in fact, be receiving at his new job. The colleagues of such persons will insist that he must have left for a personal reason (illness of his wife) or because of an unbeatable offer. To accept any other reason would imply a rejection of the department which the man is leaving, and as long as the colleague is a member of that department he is unable to accept such an explanation. Quite generally, the extent of income concealment makes any analysis of differential income subject to question.

Automation

Automation is not merely a new word for mechanization. Properly, it refers to mechanized methods for handling information. The essential element in an automated operation consists of various mechanisms for self-control in which machines feed back information on how they are doing to a computer which then makes decisions as to what shall be the next steps to be performed by the machines. Most automated operations consist of various forms for processing large amounts of data rapidly but new kinds of information handling are beginning to be used. Among these is numerical control by which it is possible to handle short runs of materials through prepunched programs available on separate tapes. When a new product or a variation on an existing product is desired, a new tape is inserted into the machinery. Another development is process control which deals with the problem of reading large numbers of dials or handling many rapid changes as in shifts in traffic on different roads or different airstrips at airports. Still another development is the information retrieval system which provides means for searching the literature in scientific areas, for editing and analysing medical statistics, and for operating translating machines. New developments undoubtedly will occur increasingly rapidly.

Among the social effects of automation, the one that has occasioned the greatest public concern has been the possible unemployment and other kinds of displacement that might occur. Certain kinds of occupations are vulnerable to possible automation, particularly those that are finally subdivided and repetitive, such as are held by factory operatives and many of the workers in filing and accounting in business offices. In the short run, the displacement may not result in an actual decline in employment because automation often is introduced not only to cut labor costs but for reasons which may produce effects other than fewer jobs. For example, automation may be introduced to expand output without adding workers in situations where those with the appropriate skills simply may not be available. This produces the result reported by many firms: they end up with as many workers as before automating and sometimes with even more. These cases of course represent submerged unemployment, since such firms would otherwise have increased their number of workers had they been available. In addition this does not provide employment for the increasing number of young people who will enter the labor market during the 1960's. A second use of automation which does not reduce the number of workers occurs when it is introduced to perform tasks of which

44

humans are incapable, such as running an automatic pilot for a jet airplane or handling radioactive materials.

In those cases where genuine displacement does occur, other social effects can be predicted. Organizations will be able to hire workers to do the new kinds of jobs available but in addition they will be confronted with the problem of whether they should retrain their present workers. The experience thus far with retraining carried on by private industry or with government help has not been very encouraging (Gursslin and Roach, 1964). There has been a low level of motivation to participate in retraining programs and there may have been a tendency for persons in charge of these programs to be overly strict in selecting program candidates. Part of the difficulty has been the tendency to see retraining as solely a psychological problem involving the acquisition of new skills. Perhaps results might be more encouraging if attention were given to the sociological effects of the loss of employment. They produce a sense of failure and a general low level of morale which can spread through an entire depressed community, making it difficult for anyone to feel that retraining offers an actual hope. In addition, in many depressed communities the more aggressive persons as well as the younger ones are likely to have left the community. Those initiating a retraining program find the population with whom they have to deal may be more than usually apathetic as well as older; they therefore have greater stakes in remaining in the community and are less willing to move to where jobs happen to be.

Another possible effect of attempting to retrain workers or of not being able to keep all of the workers on may be that the retirement and security benefit program of a company will not be as strong an incentive as it once was. If a firm is unable to offer a man long-range employment because of the possible displacement effects of automation, then any program which is based on long term proceeds, such as retirement features or other fringe benefits, will have less meaning; the company may find that it must offer more immediate attractions like higher wages or other advantages that the worker can enjoy immediately. Should there be a shrinking in labor demands, there will certainly be great pressure to encourage teen-agers to stay in school longer and for older persons to retire earlier, a trend which will produce a shortening of the work life. At the same time the number of persons at leisure increases, whether voluntarily or involuntarily, we might expect a rise in the rate of growth of entertainment and leisure industries. Some of these industries will take up the slack created by displacement elsewhere but at the same time they also are becoming mechanized.

The impact of automation on the occupational structure is difficult to predict. Some writers, such as Blauner (1962), point to the fact that many of the occupations in already automated organizations like power generation or the chemical industry require a monitoring type of activity which is more in the nature of a knack than a skill, calling for a degree of alertness and a sense of responsibility on the part of the individual. In terms of skill, such activity would probably rank no higher than semiskilled unless the worker were called upon to take action based on his observations. On the other hand, the activities of the persons who design the machines and service and repair them are certainly highly skilled, if not professional. Drucker (1957, p. 26) speculates that the factory of the future will resemble the picture presented by power generation or oil refining at the present time. Few workers are in evidence, the work having already been done in the form of machine-building and installation. Workers are called in only when a major breakdown occurs since ordinary repair work is built right into the machines, which maintain themselves. Automated operations call for programmers and controllers but the number of such persons is not likely to be large. Because of these needs for the highly trained and professional person, there surely will be pressure on universities and other educational organizations to supply them; as a result there may be mechanization of the teaching process itself in order to further increase its efficiency.

The social effects of automation will not be limited to the persons who directly man the machines but will extend to management as well. Since automation consists of many types of information controls, management will have at its disposal large amounts of data and will find itself under a strong pressure to so design the manufacturing and distribution process as to make maximum and most efficient use of the data processing apparatus. The more organized and centralized this process is, the stronger the pressure to centralize the decision-making functions themselves. Many activities now being performed by middle-level managers are likely to vanish altogether. Day-by-day decisions that revolve about the scheduling of production and the disposal of scrap can easily be programmed into a computer. One effect may be to make management into a more exacting, demanding activity since whatever can be routinized will be mechanized. This will leave to managers the task of doing only those things that machines are not able to do, such as motivating workers. Mann and Hoffman (1960, pp. 55-60) describe the case of the automation of an oil plant which resulted in a considerable increase in the power of first line foremen, in part because the second level managers were removed. If middle management is removed the question as to where top management will be derived from arises. Traditionally middle management has provided the training ground for persons who later moved into top management. If middle management should go, then the tendency to select top level managers from the outside may increase to a great extent, leading to a situation in which much of small industry may provide the sources for the management of large industry. The possibility should not be ignored that an increased use of professionally trained people may lead to more conflict between line and staff, a phenomenon already in evidence in research organizations and others employing large numbers of professionally trained persons.

An important question revolves about the probability of changes that automation may introduce in the relative power of labor and management. Since automation is likely to make some of its greatest inroads in the traditional crafts and operatives in which unionization is particularly strong the unions may be hurt, at least insofar as their strength depends upon the number of dues-paying members. It does not necessarily follow, however, that the power of management will increase as the labor unions' power decreases. When a firm automates, it turns over its production process to highly complex machinery which is very expensive to operate. This great expense leads usually to maximum utilization of the equipment over a 24-hour period. That means, in turn, that any breakdown or interruption can be financially disastrous. A study by Faunce (1958) reported that men whose jobs had been changed by automation perceived their foremen as being more tense than they had been previously, owing largely to concern about any breakdown in the operations. The result was to place the foreman and indeed the whole organization in a position of greater dependence on the line operators. The result is that although the labor unions might be hurt, the labor that does remain may be more powerful than ever, whether or not it is organized.

Some industries are more likely than others to be affected by automation. Diebold (1955) expresses the view that the manufacturing of agricultural equipment may well become much more automated but that agriculture itself is not likely to be. Buckingham (1955) forecasts automation in "continuous flow" industries such as oil refining, flour milling, and chemical production but does not believe it is likely if the product is "highly individualistic," if personal services are required, if there are special advantages in small size, or if "vast space" is needed. Such analyses are plausible but all of them assume present-day models of the processes whose future they are predicting. To rule out the possibility of automating agriculture because vast spaces are required, for example, assumes they will always be required. In view of the increased need for food on a world-wide scale and the desire of populations for a higher standard of living, we can confidently predict increase in the demand for more efficient agriculture and therefore for the use of smaller spaces than those to which we are accustomed. We already have hydroponic agriculture in which plants are grown in factories on shelves.

It similarly appears to be begging the question to rule out activities in which personal service is "needed" for this amounts to assuming that personal service will always be needed. Many activities in the area of distribution and sales which used to be carried out through personal contact between a salesman and a customer have disappeared, and we have little reason to believe that this trend will not continue. Attempts, then, to forecast the impact of automation on a particular industry or to make other predictions of such a highly detailed character are hazardous. It is difficult indeed to rule out any occupation as being inherently one which cannot be automated. The major restricting factors are likely to be need and cost.

CHAPTER 3

MANAGEMENT OF INDUSTRY

THE term "leadership," when used to describe the behavior of supervisors in industry, often refers to the attempt of the supervisors to motivate unusual work behavior beyond the minimum expectations. It has, however, a considerably wider meaning than that. Broadly, it refers to the kind of behavior that managers may engage in when the very structure of the organization requires change and when the magnitude of that change is of such a nature that there is little previous experience on which to base present judgment. In contrast to that kind of behavior, "administration" is concerned with the maintenance of the structure in operating form when the structure itself does not require any major alteration and can hence be taken for granted. Chapple and Sayles (1961) characterize such situations as those involving "deviations from normal operating conditions" (p. 64). In particular, they limit the concept to those deviations that recur often enough so that their course is predictable. Under those circumstances a manager can focus on efficiency and the reduction of costs. Such a view of organization sees it as an impersonal tool for attaining desired goals.

On the other hand, when the tool itself is no longer the appropriate one for attaining organizational goals, then it is really a matter of indifference how efficient or inefficient the tool might be: it is the tool that must be changed and this is the task of the organizational leader. Selznick (1957) sees leadership as being required even in such activities as recruitment or training when they are not methods for the routine replacement of personnel but are deliberately designed to introduce new kinds of persons into the organization in order to change its very nature. An example would be when one wishes to change the character of a business firm from one which is sales-minded to one which is production-minded. Organizational leadership thus may be called for anywhere. Nevertheless there are certain major organizational problems where leadership is particularly likely to be called for, namely in goal definition and goal implementation.

The defining of the goal ordinarily is one of the earliest problems that an organization faces. It may also become a problem in organizations which have been in existence for some time and which have actually succeeded in attaining their goals. Sills (1957) shows how the attainment of the goal of the National Foundation for Infantile Paralysis has presented that organization with a crisis. Almost without realization, it had built up a particular set of abilities, interests, and sensitivities focused about polio. On attaining its goal, it was then faced with the decision as to what should be its next move. Many of its scientists were absorbed by other organizations but the fund-raising organization itself was faced with a crisis and with the need either to disband or to shift its goals to a new disease. It discovered that it had become closely oriented to the special problems of polio and that changing its goals involved fundamental changes in the organization itself, a problem which it is still facing and which it has not completely solved.

A similar problem is faced by organizations designed to attain a major goal only once, such as an army. An army presumably is set up to attain victory. The more efficiently and effectively it does its work, however, the sooner it will attain its goal and at the same time its own disbandment. Labor unions also face a crisis when they must shift from being a fighting organization seeking recognition to being a quiet negotiating organization appropriate to the period which follows recognition. The men who led so well in the early period may be wholly inappropriate and indeed may be positively a source of difficulty in the later period.

The problems of setting goals may be so challenging and demanding that men who should be leaders may default when confronted by them. (Selznick, 1957, pp. 25-28.) Such defaults may occur because of a desire to avoid the hard work involved in setting goals or because of the wish to avoid conflict by persons who will be threatened by a definite purpose. Under those circumstances leaders may retire behind vague goals such as "readiness" or "profits," or one may get a superficial acceptance of goals where the actual goals are hidden or not talked about and the goal of the organization may be spoken of simply as "survival" without providing guidance as to how this is to be attained and at what costs. When goals are not defined the organization is likely to be characterized by a maximum of opportunism and utopianism (Selznick, 1957, pp. 74ff). A special problem is presented when a goal is clear but remains unstated. (Catton, 1962.)

Once goals have been determined they must be implemented, that is, given insurance of practical fulfillment and a special structure created which assures their attainment. The most important element in this structure is the creation and transmission of a set of values which are implied or which go along with the goals. For example, a private hospital will have not only a different set of goals but a different set of values from a teaching hospital, that is, a different set of standards for judging desirable staff behavior. Importance of values was brought out by Lipset (1950) in his description of the frustrations met by the CCF party which came to power in Saskatchewan on a Socialist program. Although the party would have preferred to create its own bureaucracy to carry out its goals, there was not time and, in addition an already trained bureaucracy was available. The use of the existing bureaucracy, it was discovered, meant that the policies of the government were entrusted to persons whose own values differed from those of the policy leaders. The bureaucracy was able to frustrate the goals of the party for long periods.

In addition to being needed in goal definition and goal implementation, organizational leadership is called for in the definition and clarification of the means whereby goals are to be attained and implemented, in problems of task assignment and coordination, motivation, and integration, and in the "sparking function." The latter refers to the need for an organization to be sparked into action, to the need for someone who knows when to press the button, for

51

someone in the army platoon to raise his hand and shout "Forward!" It is essentially a matter of timing, of sensing the moment when all factors are right, when motivation is at a maximum, supplies are available, communication is right, goals are clear, and values have been well internalized by the members. (Gross, 1961.)

An important area in which leadership is called for is that of industrialization in new countries. Some students of such industrialization, however, have taken the position that industrialism may attain essentially the same form all over the world irrespective of the particular society or culture in which it is found. Kerr, Dunlop, Harbison and Myers (1960) describe a "logic of industrialism." Wherever it occurs, they insist, industrialization uses a level of technology of great complexity. This necessitates the support of research organizations such as universities, institutes, and laboratories. In addition a wide range of skill and competence must be created. The introduction of science and other technological changes will create large scale social changes elsewhere in the society. Emphasis on individual ability will tend to make the society into much more of an open society rather than one based on caste, race, or family status.

Other students of industrialization have questioned the claim that there is a single logic of industrialism, believing instead that there may be several different roads to industrialization. Japan frequently is cited as an example of a society which succeeded in industrializing while maintaining many of the traditionalistic elements which Kerr and his colleagues suggested were incompatible with industrialization. (Belshaw, 1960, p. 106; Singer, 1960, pp. 259-263; Hoselitz, 1960, p. 228.) Insofar as the claim that there may be many roads to industrialization is true or is tenable, it is clear leadership will be called for since those building the new industry will be unable to draw on the tradition of industrialization in other countries.

Singer (1960, pp. 259-263) calls attention to the fact that the late arrivals on the industrial scene do not necessarily have to face all the problems of England or the United States in the early period of industrialization. The newer industrializing countries do not have to develop the technology from the start: they often can import it. They can use new sources of energy such as nuclear and solar energy as well as hydroelectric dams. In addition, the state, having a more important position than formerly, is likely to play a much more active role. Some of the leadership problems faced by managers in new countries has been described in selections by Harbison and Myers (1959). They also offer a framework for the examination of management, seeing it as a resource, a system of authority and a class of persons. Their study concludes that there is little evidence to support the claim that a managerial elite is gaining power in the newer countries. The power of the newer managers is counterbalanced by strong trade unions and by governments.

Social Aspects of Supervision

A strong focus of recent research has been on the effects of differing styles of supervision of work behavior and attitude. One target of the research has been the role of the foreman. Davis (1962, pp. 123-126) describes five possible roles that the foreman plays: key man in management, man in the middle, marginal man, simply another worker, and human relations specialist. Strauss (1957) points to the erosion of authority of the first-line supervisor or working supervisor occurring because of the growth in power of the foreman, because of difficulties in communication with the foreman as the latter is increasingly drawn directly from universities, and as his authority is reduced by the increased power of the union.

An important kind of research has been carried on at the Survey Research Center of the University of Michigan on the relation between supervisory practices and productivity and morale. (Likert, 1961.) A major study of office workers produced the finding that six out of nine employee-oriented supervisors were found to have high productivity in their sections in contrast to seven out of eight production-oriented supervisors, who had low productivity in their sections. In addition, it seemed that the employees were more favorably disposed towards their supervisors in the former sections (Katz, *et al.*, 1950). The conclusion that could be drawn was that the supervisor who thinks in terms of his subordinates will have higher production as well as subordinates who are more favorably disposed towards him, certainly a desirable combination.

Whyte (1961, p. 552) doubts that this conclusion can be drawn with confidence. After all, the supervisors of the sections with low productivity may by that very fact *have* to give direct attention to production rather than to employees and this close attention may well be resented because it is interpreted as pressure. In any case, subsequent studies do not confirm the office worker study completely.

Another finding of the Survey Research Center is that supervisors who practice general supervision get higher production than those who supervise closely. Another study by the Survey Research Center on a railroad section gang did not, however, confirm the finding. A study by Pelz (1952) suggested that a key variable influencing the relation between employee-orientation and degree of satisfaction with supervisor was the power that the supervisor himself had to influence his supervisors in turn. A foreman who had high power with his own superior was able to show a positive relationship between employee orientation on his part and high satisfaction with the supervisor on the part of his subordinates, a relationship which did not hold when the foreman had low power. The key factor influencing the subordinates' attitudes toward their own supervisors may therefore be the power that their superiors have to attain results when they meet with their superiors in turn. The somewhat inconclusive results of this survey work may well be due to the fact that too much is being explained on the basis of interpersonal relations. Surely the whole department or influences emanating from the whole organization must be taken into account in order to increase the accuracy of prediction (Whyte, 1961, pp. 556-557).

Blau and Scott (1962, pp. 151-153) report findings that do not support the conclusions of the Survey Research Center group on closeness of supervision. In the case of two social work agencies they studied, work group productivity was not found to be related to authoritarianism. In explanation they suggest that perhaps a service organization, in contrast to a factory or private office, is of such a nature that employees will not react to supervision they find unpleasant by reducing their productivity. Their strong orientation as professionals to doing the best possible job they can will come out in spite of the working conditions they may face. Blau and Scott (1962, pp. 153-159) also describe studies which deal with other aspects of supervisor-subordinate relationships. They find that emotional detachment, consistency, and hierarchical interdependence — dimensions ignored by many researchers — are closely related to the ability of a supervisor to command the loyalty of his subordinates. This in turn was related to productivity, since apparently supervisors who had won the loyal support of their subordinates were most successful in securing willing compliance with their directives and in stimulating interests among their subordinates.

An important concept in traditional management analysis has been the span of control — the number of persons who should be supervised by any one manager. Worthy, reporting on his studies in the Sears Roebuck organization, concluded that flat organizations (those in which a large number of subordinates report to a manager) have higher productivity and contribute a larger share of persons with management potential to the organization than do tall organizations. He attributes these results to the fact that when the manager of a store with a flat organization is faced with the task of supervising the work of some 30 department managers he cannot possibly supervise each of them closely. Instead he will be forced to let each run his department in his own way. A manager permitted to do that will develop initiative (if he has any ability at all) and hence further his managerial potential because he must, in effect, train himself. On the other hand, tall orgnizations exhibit the situation in which the store manager will supervise about six second level supervisors who in turn will each supervise some six department managers. Each of these managers will give close supervision to his subordinate with the result that his subordinate will not develop his own initiative but instead will refer important decisions to his superior.

Whyte (1961, pp. 91-92) suggests that Worthy's results may apply in only certain situations. He points to the importance of the fact that, in the Sears stores in which flat organization was found to be more efficient, the departments are essentially independent of one another. Should the shoe department be poorly operated, no adverse effects will be suffered by the drug department. In time the poor management will come to the attention of the store manager through cost reports or in other ways, and he can take appropriate action. Such insulation of departments from each other obviously is not the case in a factory in which the poor management of a department such as the paint department spreads out its effects in the form of poorly painted parts, and hence may bring the entire production process to a halt. In such a situation another level of supervision will be required to relate the paint department to the department that makes use of its output or that sends parts to it. Similar problems arise in situations where technology is complex or where it may be impossible or difficult to measure the results of a particular department and therefore to attribute changes in cost or income to that department alone. In spite of Whyte's criticisms, research of this kind casts doubt on traditional assumptions that one can simply reason out mathematically the proper number of persons a supervisor should direct. Research will have to be turned to for answers and unquestionably the number for most efficient supervision will vary from situation to situation.

Managerial Succession

An important kind of research has dealt with the effects on the organization of changes in managers. A study by Gouldner (1954) of a gypsum plant and a study by Guest (1962, b) of an automobile plant can be compared. In the Gouldner study, the replacement of one manager by another resulted in sharp increases in tension and stress and a decline in performance. In the automobile plant results were more positive: costs decreased, output went up, there was less absenteeism and turnover, few labor grievances and other improvements. Peel (the new manager in the gypsum plant) faced problems which Cooley (the new manager in the automobile plant) did not have to face. In the former case, it had become the tradition to promote from within the organization, a tradition which had not been followed in the appointment of Peel, who had been brought in from the outside. Consequently, the legitimacy of Peel's succession was questionable. Second, the manager who preceded Peel left behind him a group of men loyal to him personally. He had created an 'indulgency pattern" in which persons were permitted considerable latitude in deviating from the rules. Peel could not count on the transfer of this loyalty to him when he took over.

By contrast the men in the automobile plant had been accustomed to changes in managers because they took place fairly often. In addition it was a custom to bring in managers from other plants. There was no sense of close association between the manager and subordinates. When Cooley entered he thus was not breaking any precedent nor did he find a number of persons loyal to his predecessor. Since Peel found such a group to be present, however, and since he could not count on the loyalty of this group to provide him with information on what was going on in the plant through informal means, he was forced to tighten up the control and impose formal rules as a way of securing predictable behavior; this meant destroying the indulgency pattern which had formally existed. Cooley did not have such a tradition to worry about and instead instituted a series of meetings in which he assumed the role of learner. Actually, Cooley's predecessor behaved very much like Peel. He had maintained a rigid, tight rule-enforcing kind of organization; therefore it was quite easy for his successor to relax the rules. The results support the claim that it is much easier for a supervisor to replace a man who has maintained a tight organization than one who has maintained relatively loose controls, even though the latter system may be more efficient or may result in workers with higher morale.

Size of organization and the relative size of the administrative component may also be related to problems presented by succession. Though the evidence is not conclusive, the data tend to support the assertion that as organizations increase in size their complexity also increases (Anderson and Warkov, 1961). Caplow (1957) offers data which indicate that the greater the size of the organization the greater its stability. Taking these data into account, Grusky (1961) draws our attention to the fact that most studies of organizational succession have been concerned with quite small organizations. The problems that have occurred may therefore be peculiar to small organizations and not be found in larger ones. Using data provided by *Fortune* magazine on the 500 largest corporations in the United States, Grusky took the top 26 and the bottom 27 of those corporations as his sample of large and small firms. He secured data on changes in the names listed in the key jobs in the firm from 1949 to 1959. His data show that frequency of succession at the top was positively related to size of firm, a result which held even when age of the managers was held constant. This result suggests that the greater bureaucratization in the larger firms acts to cushion the otherwise disruptive consequences of succession.

In contrast the chief executive in the small unbureaucratized firm is more likely to be the founder or one of his relatives and to be closely identified with the organization as a whole. When such a key person leaves there will be distinctly unsettling consequences. The highly bureaucratized firms are more likely to be staffed by professional managers who routinize the succession process through rules regulating retirement, rotation and promotion of officials. In such a situation succession is much more common and prepared for and hence not so disrupting. In a further test of Grusky's generalization on a sample of heads of state public health departments, state community and/or institutional mental health programs, local public health departments and local mental health departments or centers, Kriesberg (1962) confirms Grusky's conclusion. Hughes (1956) distinguishes between what he calls "itinerant" and "home-guard" career lines as follows: "The home-guard are the people who make their careers with little or no itinerancy; the itinerants progress by moving from one place or institution to another" (Hughes, 1956, p. 25). Kriesberg (1962, pp. 356-357) suggests that perhaps the larger departments that he studied are most likely to recruit itinerants (persons who will have national reputations) who then will advance by moving to new places or institutions. The likelihood of succession is hence related to the career pattern. Large organizations attract persons to whom succession or movement from one organization to another is entirely appropriate to the sorts of careers that they exhibit and therefore is not so stressful. Levenson (1961) further develops this theme by showing that organizations will anticipate succession by training persons to take over their superior's position. Succession must be prepared for, or the organization may face too many crises. This very preparation may itself create problems, however, since the company will not be able to promote *all* of the persons whom it has been training.

Relations Among Managers

One of the most important changes that has taken place in the organization of management has been the growth of staff organizations to render assistance to line or production organizations. The legal department is created to advise in the handling of patents, a division of inspection to check the quality of goods, a department of purchasing is given the responsibility for centralizing the securing of all supplies from outside sellers. The advisory function is not necessarily that of staff or line. Etizioni (1959) points out that in hospitals, for example, the role of staff and line may be reversed, for the positions who perform the "productive" activity of curing patients are members of the professional staff and are not a part of the line organization of the hospital. Strauss and Sayles (1960, pp. 397-399) describe the changes that have been undergone by the personnel department in organizations. In the earliest period their activities were limited to keeping records. In the 1920's employees' services became important in response to new theories of industrial relations and to the attempt to offset union organization drives and the feared Russian revolution. The response of the managers was to increase paternalism by providing cafeterias, company stores, counselors and other benefits. During the 1930's the department began to take greater responsibility for all employee and union relations, taking upon itself the major responsibility for hiring, firing, wage determination, handling union grievances, transfers and promotions. In unionized plants some members of personnel departments became full-time negotiators while others spent their time justifying promotions or other planned changes to the union. Still others were put in charge of developing fringe benefit programs in response to union pressures for them.

One effect of the growth of the power of the personnel department was a reduction in the power of the line supervisor, who found that his former freedom to hire, fire, or discipline and handle grievances had been greatly reduced. He was still likely, however, to be blamed for employee discontent even though his power to remedy such discontent had been abridged. In this new situation the personnel department as well as other staff departments found that they were called upon to give advice and counsel to the line. This, however, creates a dilemma, for how can a staff department be expected to help a line supervisor make important decisions and at the same time maintain harmonious relationships with him? (Gross, 1964.) Theoretically the personnel department provides information and advice which the line then uses to make a decision. Such a distinction is not realistic, since the person receiving the "advice" is in the position of being able to ignore it only at his peril. The advisor is, in fact, the person who is making the decision *for* the line supervisor. The staff of personnel, being experts, also will have access to knowledge which the line manager does not have and the staff will have a natural desire to apply this knowledge. It is therefore easy for them to slip from their advisory role into a decision-making role. The resulting dependence is the basis of increasing power. (Emerson, 1962.)

Dalton (1950) drawing upon research which he did in three large manufacturing organizations, presents a picture of continuous line-staff conflict. Staff personnel were an ambitious, restless, mobile group. This was due in part to their age, which usually was younger than that of line personnel. In addition their younger age made line personnel more reluctant to accept instructions from them. Staff persons, with their better educations, fully expected that the learning and the knowledge that this implied would itself carry authority. The formal hierarchy of statuses in staff departments did not offer very great opportunities for mobility. A member of a staff department soon discovered that if he wished to move up in the company the only way he could do so would be by moving over into a line position. This required being able to get along with line personnel, who then would request such a transfer. Another source of conflict revolved around the fact that staff persons were highly status conscious, expressing this consciousness in emphasis on dress, appearance, and other items of "front." Staff persons often were feared or disliked by line persons because, by definition, staff persons were supposed to introduce change and other innovations into the organization. Line personnel often feared being "shown up" for not having thought of these changes themselves or were concerned lest the changes in methods or personnel would reduce their own authority, expose forbidden practices or departmental inefficiency.

In such a situation then, staff and line people found that they were mutually dependent on one another. The staff needed the line in order to move ahead in the company. The line needed the staff in order to protect their positions. The cases of successful line-staff relations are those in which the departments "accommodated" to each other, which sometimes resulted in an actual violation of company policies and subversion of standards. In another work Dalton (1959) focuses attention on conflict among the line officers themselves. The most effective managers, he found, were those who were goal-oriented rather than method oriented. These persons fought continually for the expansion of their departments in part to increase their own power and in part to help attain departmental objectives. Since such expansion usually led to disputes, many power struggles developed in which the less aggressive managers and their departments lost out. Contrary to the views of many, Dalton sees such power struggles as entirely functional for organizational change, since without them organizations would be too slow to adjust to new conditions. The picture presented by Dalton contrasts sharply with the picture drawn by W. H. Whyte (1956) of the "organization man" bent on getting along with his fellows.

Blau and Scott (1962, pp. 175-176) discuss an unpublished study by Crozier of the French tobacco industry. Crozier found that maintenance workers were highly satisfied with their jobs, production workers less so, and supervisors quite dissatisfied. A similar pattern was evident at the higher managerial levels where technical engineers were found to be more satisfied than top managers. Crozier interprets these results as implying that bureaucracy has the effect of eliminating many areas of uncertainty and consequently power will accrue to persons who can control the remaining areas of uncertainty. In the tobacco plants, the main area of uncertainty was what to do in case of machine breakdown. The maintenance workers and engineers therefore found that their power increased and with that their satisfaction with their jobs. Crozier sees expertness as an alternative to authority that becomes manifest in

61

areas that are not completely bureaucratized. The power that rests on such expertness in areas of uncertainty is inherently unstable, however, since the very success of the specialist in handling an area of uncertainty is soon likely to lead to the routinization and bureaucratization of his procedures.

CHAPTER 4

INDUSTRIAL ORGANIZATION: THE VIEW FROM INSIDE

Types of Organization

IT is possible to classify industrial organizations in many different ways. Blauner, after pointing to a tendency for studies of organization to be biased in favor of certain kinds of organizations (Blauner, 1962, p. 8), suggests that organizations should be classified in terms of technology, ranging from the most complex to the most mechanized and automated. Etzioni (1961) proposes a typology which goes beyond industrial organizations. His typology is based on the compliance structure — coercive (such as prisons and mental hospitals), utilitarian (businesses), and normative (such as churches). Other classifications are based on the extent to which an organization may be manned by volunteers, employees, or conscripts; the type of institutional area in which the organization operates (economic, political, religious, etc.); the type of decision-making strategy employed (Thompson and Tuden, 1959); the distinction between production and service, and on the criterion of who benefits from the organization — the customer, the members of the organization themselves, or society (Blau and Scott, 1962, pp. 42-57). We shall adopt a classification here which reflects the actual practices in the studies that have been made of industrial organizations. These can be put into three categories: bureaucratic, collegial, and paternalistic.

The bureaucratic organizations make up the bulk of industrial studies. They are well illustrated by manufacturing firms and have been described in terms of the characteristics of bureaucracy outlined by Max Weber, the major German sociologist — specialization, hierarchical coordination, the dependence on rules, and impersonality. The structure is divided into a technical and social organization. The technical organization in turn consists of two kinds of sub-organizations — shop and engineering. The shop carries on the line activity that is the manufacturing process or the service that firm provides. The engineering organization plans the shop's technical procedures and the tools and machinery it uses. In reality the two kinds of organizations may overlap. One may find a chemist or an engineer in the line to assist the shop with its technical problems and, in turn, engineering organizations may become so large that they include persons who perform shop activities, such as drawing up blue-prints, photography, etc., for the engineering departments.

The formal *social* organization of the firm consists of three interlocking organizations: the supervisory organization, the line organization, and the staff organization. The supervisory organization makes up the formal authority structure, that is, each person reports directly to a superior and is responsible to him. Each superior usually will have several subordinates reporting to him. The result of this organization is the familiar branching type of organization one sees on the standard company organization charts. Orders and information are expected to flow along these lines. In addition to the formal organization one may have a labor union which cuts across this organization and does not include supervisors. The whole structure is pulled together through a communication network which includes face-to-face communication, non-face-to-face oral communication (telephone, interoffice communication), and written communication. These types of communication will have important differences in results. Communication over the telephone thus must be carried without the assistance one usually gets from the gestures with which persons communicate to each other. In written communication, besides having to wait a considerable length of time for a reply, it is even possible that there will be no reply at all, a situation which is rare or is regarded as insulting in interpersonal communication.

The direction of the communication may be significant for its impact on persons in the organization. In vertical communication, orders go down the line from supervisors and information is gathered in lower levels and transmitted upward. The significant element here is the extent to which orders are altered as they go down to take account of special conditions. Information is similarly altered or interpreted and generalized as it moves up so that persons high up in the organization often may have only a very general idea of what is going on at the very bottom. This places them in a state of great dependence on their subordinates. Of particular importance are cost control and union information, since they do not go up the line step by step to be altered by each supervisor in the light of conditions known to him or in the light of the need to compress information. Such information is gathered at the bottom, summarized, mimeographed and then distributed simultaneously to several levels higher up. Consequently it may not become known to the first or second line supervisors until their supervisors call them with a demand for an explanation as to why costs have gone up or why a grievance is being made by the union. Such information therefore puts great pressure on them and they will be forced to spend a good deal of their time trying to anticipate and prepare for information.

Horizontal communication also may become extremely complicated. Theoretically, interaction between persons on the same level is supposed to take place through a common supervisor. In fact, this procedure is so time consuming that short cuts directly across, bypassing the supervisor, will occur with the result that the information will be kept from him. Such short cuts, however, appear to be the dominant pattern reported in a study of a spinning department by Simpson (1959). Whether such horizontal interaction will take place depends on the structure as well as on the nature of interpersonal relationships. For example, if a shop is concerned with assembly of a part it will have horizontal relationships with only those departments that supply it with the materials it needs and those departments to which it delivers materials when it is finished. On the other hand a rivet or paint shop which performs a service for a large number of departments may present an altogether different picture. A paint shop will find itself forced to deal with many departments, each with special needs or special demands. There consequently may be much more tension and conflict between such a department and other departments and the activity itself may call for a higher degree of foremanship skill than otherwise would be the case.

The bureaucratic form of organization has been subjected to a great deal of criticism. In particular the admirers of this form of organization have tended to underestimate its possible harmful effects especially on those who get carried away by emphasis on rules or who use the impersonality in order to hide behind the organization and protect their own deficiencies. In spite of those defects, however, it remains the most efficient method for the accomplishment of large-scale work tasks that has yet been discovered.

Examples of collegial organizations are committees that have a task assignment, a case conference, a university department, a research and development organization in industry, and many kinds of craft and professional associations. Sociologically-oriented research on task-oriented groups has been concerned with the kind of roles which persons bring with them to such meetings and the kind of roles they assume at the meetings. This is based on the sociological observation that each person's behavior is related to the role expectations he has and others have of him and that in time such expectations lead to a stable structure in a small group. The roles which persons assume at meetings have been described by Beane and Sheats (1948) as content roles (initiator, information seeker, blocker, expert, etc.), and process roles (summarizer, task-setter, encourager, mediator, playboy, etc.). The research has examined the productivity of groups in which the chairman plays both content and process roles as compared to those in which he limits himself to a process role and hence plays a more democratic role.

At one time a good deal of research was conducted on leaderless groups. Maier and Solem (1952) recorded results which showed that groups with formal leaders were better at solving mathematical problems than those without because formal leaders made sure that minority opinions were expressed and often these were the correct ones. In a group without such a leader the majority opinion would act as a pressure to such a minority to keep quiet, and consequently the correct result might never be heard. After careful examination of the research in this area, Blau and Scott conclude as follows: "By providing social support, challenging stimulation, error correction, and a *laissez-faire* competition for respect among participants, the free flow of communication contributes to finding solutions to problems, to making decisions, and to creative thinking. But the battle ground of ideas generated by such a free flow makes coordination more difficult." (1962, p. 139.) In effect, then, one might have to pay for securing control and coordination by giving up some of the potentially fruitful results of allowing a free flow of information in such a group.

Comparing construction and mass-production industries in the United States, Stinchcombe (1959) finds that the former are much less bureaucratized than the latter although they are just as rationalized. The result is due in part to the seasonal variations in the construction industry and in part to the greater professionalization of its labor force. As a consequence it can do without much of the administrative staffing required by mass industry. A similar argument may apply to many kinds of professional organizations also. A combination of the collegial and bureaucratic form of organization can be seen in research and development organizations in industry which consist of a group of peers who are expected to work towards a definite research goal according to a schedule and under direction. Howton (1963) tells us that in order to be able to avoid "dirty work" (work that is considered demeaning or hurtful to the professional self-image), a group of scientists he observed had to spend a great deal of their time making certain that their work assignments were acceptable to them, which actually left them with little time in which to do the work itself.

In organizations employing large numbers of professional persons such as scientists, mathematicians, psychologists, or others with advanced training, the specialist form of organization is common. In this type of collegial organization, one brings persons with similar training together under a leader or manager who himself is a member of a profession. One thus may have a group of chemists working together under the direction of a chemist. This type of organization is much preferred by professional persons since it enables them to work on problems of professional importance, it means that their work is evaluated by persons in whom they have confidence, communication is likely to be free and easy and morale is likely to be high. The danger, however, is that professionals will be carried away by their own concerns and neglect the organizational problems for whose solution they have been hired. In addition they may become highly insulated from the rest of the organization and not be responsive to attempts to influence their thinking (Kornhauser, 1962).

In recent years an alternative form of organization for such professionals, the task force (Wickesberg and Cronin, 1962), has been used in some cases. In this type of organization persons of different backgrounds are brought together and given a particular job to do with a target date for its completion. One may have a task force composed of a chemist, a physicist, a mathematician, a man skilled in systems, and others who have a particular kind of experience, all under the direction of a manager who is keenly conscious of the organizational requirements for the task. As the theoretical problems are overcome, the group can shift to production problems, adding production people for that purpose. Later these may be dropped and persons skilled in sales and other activities appropriate to the new stage of development of the project will be brought in. When the target has been attained, the group is disbanded. This form of organization sometimes has been used with startling success, as in the case of the Polaris missile at the Minneapolis Honeywell organization. Its advocates often are enthusiastic and those who have been with such a group may be high in praise of the possible results which may be attained. It also, however, presents serious problems. A major problem is that of coordination. Since one has persons of different backgrounds and since these persons are highly trained, usually with strong conceptions of their own importance, unusually skilled leadership is required to get such persons to work together. Each may regard the other with suspicion and may underestimate the possible contribution of the other's specialty. If one person is from a specialty which has generally higher prestige (for example, a physician in a group of social workers) he will expect greater deference even though his knowledge may be no more relevant than that of someone else.

A problem often arises as to who is to be given credit and how credit is to be assigned for the accomplishment of the task force. The leader may find others attempting to undercut his position or feeling that he is taking a greater share of credit than he deserves. Since the work of professionals is very difficult to evaluate except by other professionals, such a group creates a situation in which men are appraised by persons outside their own specialty, an evaluation which they are likely to reject. Another problem is the source of recruitment of the members of the task force and what happens to them afterwards. In large organizations, it may be possible to draw upon persons in other departments. Obviously the other department then must do without that person's services, an activity which is possible in an expanding market where substitutes are available. After a project is over, persons may return to departments in which they were formerly located only to find that the jobs have changed, perhaps greatly, and that they are being "carried" by the company. Some firms have turned to the "elite task force" idea in which they hire their personnel from outside organizations which maintain pools of specialized talent. Such an approach does not really solve the problem since one is not at all sure that the persons in such organizations have the capabilities required. In addition, this approach means bringing into the organization outsiders over whom one has no control and exposing company affairs and secrets to them.

Paternalistic forms of industrial organization often emerge from a feudal tradition in which the lord of the manor had responsibility for the welfare of the residents in return for their loyalty and their services. Kerr, *et al.* (1960) find this form of organization quite common in countries in the beginning stages of industrial development. In small establishments, the proprietor will use his own relatives as workers; this will enable the family to remain intact as the society begins the process of industrialization. Management provides many services for reasons other than those stemming from societal expectations. A firm may provide lunches if and when it discovers that the efficiency of its employees is low because of malnutrition. Similarly where a company must attract persons to isolated locations, as in oil production or sugar plantations, it will be forced to provide housing in order to secure workers. Paternalism is important in many organizations in the United States as well and it is of course the major form of organization for the approximately 85 per cent of all United States firms which are small businesses, many dependent on some type of family help.

Transforming Persons Into Members: Teaching and Learning

Teaching and learning not only are means whereby persons acquire skills or ideas which are related to work performance, but also are means whereby persons assume the status of industrial colleague. Consequently, particular interest focuses on the standards and values to which students in training — whether in a separate educational setting or on the job itself — are exposed. At the same time it is recognized that one of the most important controls of the make-up of work colleague groups can be provided by restricting the number who are permitted to learn the occupational skills. We shall examine each of these two controls in the would-be worker, considering first techniques for restricting the number permitted to learn.

Restrictions on entry to the learning situation may be either formal or informal. Formal restrictions include such devices as prerequisites before one may enter dental, law, or engineering schools. The sheer length of the occupational education itself will stop many persons even after they have begun their course of study. Many occupations require internships, and there are good and poor internships. A Negro physician may be prevented from entering practice on the same level as a white by failing to secure an internship in a good hospital. Where much of the learning must take place on the job still other devices are used. The factory personnel office screens persons and the union may use the hiring hall or the closed shop, if legal, or exercise other controls upon the hiring process. This becomes a circular process whereby persons are unable to learn the skills the job requires except by taking a job and are unable to secure the job because they do not have the skills. Informal criteria include race, religion, age, and sex and they may

70

be applied in various ways. A popular technique is the informal quota in the schools. Another device is the use of a performance test, as in dentistry. As is well known the required photograph on the application form may be used to restrict Negroes.

In addition to controlling entry powerful controls are present in the learning situation itself. Where the learning consists in part of formal education off the job, control is exercised by having accepted members of the occupation do the teaching. Accountants teach accounting students, and engineers teach engineering students. There thus is assurance that appropriate attitudes are being transmitted along with skills.

The most important control on learning is that which occurs *on* the job itself, a statement that seems to remain true regardless of how much formal education the occupation requires. The things learned on the job are of three kinds: regular technical skills, tricks of the trade, and social skills.

The teaching of regular technical skills is distinguished from the teaching of such skills off-the-job by the realism of the on-the-job situation. In addition, a great deal of the learning is informal so that persons may be unaware of the fact that it is taking place until some time has lapsed. This in turn may easily lead to the growth of myths about the length of time required to produce a skilled member of the trade. A striking example is the myth of the boy apprentice in the building trades.

By a "trick of the trade" we mean a device which saves a person from his own mistakes. The most important are tricks that save time, save energy, and prevent a man's being hurt. All occupations have their share of shortcuts and a part of the efficiency of experienced workers can be attributed to them. In some occupations, one must learn how to lift heavy weights without strain; in others one learns to avoid cutting oneself or hitting one's thumb with a hammer. Matthews (1950) has described how a rookie fireman must learn never to look up when scaling a ladder lest burning material fall on his face. The fireman learns also to put on his helmet before he buttons his firemen's coat so that if he falls off the "rig" his head will be protected. In addition he learns to change from his street shoes to his firemen's boots one shoe at a time, so that if the alarm should go off he will never have more than one shoe left to put on.

Perhaps the most ingenious is the trick of the "smoke eater," one who can stay in a smoke-filled room for a long time by getting breaths of fresh air from the nozzle of the hose before water is pumped through it. Sutherland (1937, pp. 44-45) has described the trick of the pickpocket of stationing himself right next to a sign saying "Beware of pickpockets" because of the tendency of persons, on reading the sign, to feel for their wallets, thus notifying the pickpocket where the wallets are kept.

Last are social skills. The worker must learn how to get along with fellow workers. To do this he must learn what their social world and code are. One of the commonest ways of teaching social skills is by horseplay, including all the legendary devices for making the novice look foolish: tripping him as he passes, hiding his tools, sending him out for a nonexistent tool. Such devices have the definite function of letting the individual know that there is a group and that the individual cannot regard himself as a member of the team until he has been accepted by that group. Acceptance, in turn, means learning how to behave. The individual must learn what is considered to be a good day's work and to restrict his output to that point. He must learn when to keep his mouth shut and what it is safe to talk about. He must learn to whom he can talk and whom he must avoid. The importance of these considerations led Merton and his colleagues, in their intensive study of the student physician, to describe the process of learning in terms of socialization, the process by which persons "selectively acquire the values and attitudes, the interest, skills and knowledge — in short, the culture — current in the groups in which they are, or seek to become a member." (Merton, *et al.*, 1957, p. 287.)

On the other hand, Becker, *et al.* (1961) dispute the socialization approach, maintaining instead that medical students do not take on a professional role while they are students largely because the system they operate in does not allow them to do so. Students are made painfully aware of the fact that they are students, that they know very little and that they can only play at being doctors. Instead students are forced to come to terms with the immediate problem of pleasing their instructors and of doing well in medical school if they wish to be physicians. There remains, however, no question that values — in this case the culture of the student group — must be learned. If members of an occupation interact with each other very much and develop an occupational subculture it is likely to be expressed in the form of an argot, an occupational language which, together with functioning as a means for efficient communication, serves as a device to recognize the members of the occupation and by that token those who can be trusted.

Systems of Work Control

There are two main kinds of work controls: those that come from within the work situation — folkways, mores, and sanctions — and those that come from outside. In any new work situation there is considerable floundering around at first. Since persons do not know which situations are likely to recur, they do not know which ones should be subjected to group control and definition. Gradually, however, they come to know what to expect of one another. Bendix (1956, pp. 203-204) has described this process in the early industrial period in England. It took a considerable length of time, he points out, for workers to develop what he calls "an internalized ethic of work performance." Gradually folkways and mores develop that define duties and obligation. Among occupations with pretensions to becoming professions, one gets a code. The code often is formal and as such may get further and further away from the actual work situation until it becomes a creed or faith, a statement of that by which occupational members are supposed to live. Such a code functions as an *apologia* which states what the industry does for the world and justifies its contribution. In back of this code there is a real working code; it is this that usually is more significant. Laymen sometimes feel that the creed was once lived up to and the working code is a departure from it. This view is a fallacy because in life action precedes words, and the working code is usually much tougher than the formal code.

Sanctions may be imposed in many ways. One of the best is to make it appear that the sanction is coming from the outside — like the old school-boy technique of punishing a fellow-pupil by getting him in bad with the teacher. The rate-buster may find rejected pieces slipping into his work pile, or the group may work at top speed in order to cause the rate-buster to get behind in his work. As the pieces pile up on his desk, the foreman appears and wonders about him. The man will, ironically, get a reputation for being a slow worker and may be shifted out of the work group to another one.

These are informal sanctions. There are, of course, formal sanctions. The individual may be rejected from the occupation: the priest may be excommunicated or reprimanded or unfrocked, the lawyer may be disbarred. These things happen but they are much less common than informal exclusion from an inner circle. If legal sanctions are applied at all, they are likely to come from a group outside the professional body altogether. Informal sanctions are applied first and formal sanctions only if the person gets very far out of line. In most professions the device of referral is a major source of clients. One of the ways one can hurt an individual is to stop referring clients to him. This is a powerful informal control. At the same time, in order to work effectively the person must identify with the group, that is, his status in the work group must be his most important status. If the person has an *escape* into another status, then group sanctions may not hurt him much. The best illustrations of those with status escapes are minority groups: Negroes, Jews, Mexicans, Japanese, women. It is possible for members of minority groups to escape the impact of group sanctions if they believe that the sanction is being imposed on them because of their minority group membership rather than because of their group membership. The question is: Who can insult you? To be an insult it must hurt. Only if a person values the opinion of the group will he be very much upset if the group disapproves of his behavior.

Controls from outside the work situation include those from clients, other professions and occupations, and public opinion in general. Such control is typically mediated through an authority structure (for example, work duties of electricians employed in a factory), the market price mechanism (charges self-employed electricians are able to collect for their services), governmental controls (the building code, licensing), and the general control of custom (few electricians would refuse to respond to an urgent night call from a householder whose electricity had failed for no obvious reason). Nonoccupational controls are particularly strong among the professions yet no occupation escapes some control. We allow the playwright and actor some license to satirize society and be risqué, but the censor is never far away.

Controls in industrial organizations may take a variety of forms that are related to the kind of organization one is examining. Blau and Scott (1962, pp. 169-170) point out that, in the welfare agencies that they studied, the work of case workers was continually interrupted by emergency requests from clients and by supervisors who felt free to disrupt their work when they thought it necessary. Much less of this sort of behavior occurred as one moved further up the line. Jaques (1956) has analyzed the time between interruptions or, more generally, between evaluations of employee performance, feeling that this time provides a measure of responsibility. He finds that financial rewards are correlated with the relative span of discretionary responsibility. Also affecting the way in which work is evaluated are physical factors such as the distance separating the supervisor from the subordinate. Clark (1958, pp. 71-72) suggests that the geographical dispersion of the many centers of adult education in a metropolitan area gave the officials more autonomy than they otherwise might have had.

Of importance in industrial organization are impersonal mechanisms of control. These have been examined by Walker and Guest (1952; 1956) in their studies of assembly line production. Where one installs an assembly line, the need for close supervision is removed because the line itself dictates the pace of work. The foreman spends his time assisting men who are having difficulty since the latter are unable to leave the line. The foreman consequently may not be perceived as exercising close supervision. In automated operations one might expect a further reduction in the closeness of supervision but this result is not in fact what happens, as researches by Faunce (1958) and Walker (1957) have shown. Blau and Scott (1962, pp. 181-183) interpret this finding as meaning that as long as automation is not accompanied by a higher level of skill, it will not result in increased discretion. On the other hand a study by Blauner (1962) of a chemical firm in the Bay area of California reported a reduction in closeness of supervision and a greater sense of worker responsibility although they were

75

not noticeably higher skilled persons. Blauner casts doubt on the usefulness of the concept of "skill" for operators in automated structures, preferring to look upon such operators as "responsible" for chemical or other processes. He finds that these workers do not feel that the machines are "controlling" them.

CHAPTER 5

CAREERS

Career Selection

SOME students of work place a great deal of emphasis on the wide range available to youngsters and find, not surprisingly, that the jobs persons actually end up with may differ from those they earlier expressed a desire to enter. The existence of such indeterminacy obviously makes prediction hazardous. This indeterminacy, plus the large amount of job shifting which persons go through, leads some analysts to introduce "accident" as an explanation for the jobs people get. (Cuber and Kenkel, 1954, p. 301; Miller and Form, 1951, p. 651.) Such factors, however, hardly constitute explanations. In many cases they are rationalizations after the fact because the person himself is not aware of the factors motivating him. In any case the question is why these "accidental" or "trivial" occurrences affect some and not others. In the case of a student who goes to a vocational school because "someone" has told him automobile mechanics make high wages, why is it that another student who hears the same story does not transfer schools? It may be that the "someone" did not get a chance to tell him to begin with. Everyone is exposed to accidental occurrences and contacts and therefore we must ask why some apparently are in a state of readiness to respond and others are not. The problem is one of selectivity.

A major selective force is the "cultural perspective," that is, the process by which a culture channels the occupational ambitions of its young by limiting the alternatives available and endowing some with higher values than others. Occupations have differing amounts of prestige, a fact which is related to the cultural emphases and values. The effect is that of holding up certain occupations as more worthy of pursuit than others. Any occupational scale, then, is not only a record of differential rank but also a crude picture of the values of the society and the directions in which young persons are being encouraged to go. The North-Hatt scale may hence be regarded as a picture of societal values. In addition, the investigators specifically asked the sample why they had rated a job as they had with the following results: (National Opinion Research Center, 1953, p. 418.)

The job pays so well	18%
It serves humanity; it is an essential job	16%
Preparation requires much education, hard work and money	14%
The job carries social prestige	14%
It requires high moral standards, honesty, responsibility	9%
It requires intelligence and ability	9%
It provides security, steady work	5%
The job has a good future; the field is not overcrowded	3%
The job is pleasant, safe, and easy	2%
It affords maximum chance for initiative and freedom less than	.5%
Miscellaneous answers, don't know; no answer	10%

It is interesting to note that although amount of pay heads the list, that category does not dwarf any other; indeed no category does, a fact suggestive of lack of emphasis in our society on any one particular goal. On the other hand, Taft (1953) reports that an Australian sample felt that the status of an occupation depended most on the required amount of education, intelligence, the interest of the work, and its importance to the community, and depended least on size of income, working conditions, and stability. This underlines the importance of cultural variation.

The foregoing discussion relates to the culture as a whole. No one, however, participates entirely in all of the culture. As a consequence, his cultural perspective is considerably narrower than has been indicated thus far. Special attention attaches to the role of the family, physical location, sex and age, education and social class, on each of which we shall comment briefly.

It is not surprising to learn that a considerable part of an individual's job horizon is defined for him by his family. A major question is how many occupations the individual's family knows about or is sympathetic toward. A child's father knows only his own and a few related occupations, and it is these occupations to which the growing child is exposed. It makes a difference to his ambition pattern whether the voices from the living room that he listens to in bed (when he should be asleep) are those of successful lawyers or of successful pickpockets. Only in occupations about which his father and his friends know is the child likely to receive assistance or even understanding. This process, after many generations, produces the ethnic and religious concentrations in certain occupations in industries which, although often much exaggerated, do exist: Italians in the fruit and vegetable business and in the needle trades; Eastern European Jewish persons in retail business and the professions; Japanese in fishing; and the Irish on the police force. Here is a powerful restriction, which operates from within, on the individual's career goals. He is effectively prevented from entering by the fact that the group in which he grows up does not know about the occupation, does not understand it, or is unsympathetic towards it. This situation places an additional burden on him who would enter such an occupation: he must fight his own group. Important also are social class splits *within* the same family where father and mother may have differentially valued occupations. (Watson and Barth, 1964.)

Occupational inheritance is a continuing theme in analyses of social mobility but it is also relevant to an understanding of the role of the family in occupational selection. On the whole most studies confirm each other in the finding that there is a strong tendency for a son to be found in the same occupational category as his father. The picture varies, however, for different occupations. Rogoff (1953, pp. 118, 119, and 57) found actual inheritance of occupation, compared to expected, particularly high for professionals and semiprofessionals, proprietors, unskilled, protective service, personal service, and those in farming. The National Opinion Research Center (1953) study found that the percentage of the sample in the same occupation as the father ranged from a low of 8 per cent for domestic and personal service workers to a high of 84 per cent for farmers. It was particularly high for businessmen and skilled workers. Duncan and Hodge (1963), in a careful regression analysis of a Chicago sample, conclude that the volume of total inheritance of father's occupation is not very impressive and that education is a better predictor of occupation of son. Another factor of importance in inheritance is the presence of a proprietarial element as illustrated by such industries as farming, in retail stores, service enterprises, small factories, sales agencies, truck agencies, and commercial schools. In these some relatively concrete thing is present which can be handed on intact to the next generation, especially if the inheriting son has become known to and accepted by steady customers. The content of what is transmitted is also of importance. It is one thing to teach one's son a specific craft, juggling, for example, but another thing to transmit drives, ambitions or a set of attitudes. (Faris, 1947.) Of particular importance is the transmission of a belief in the desirability of attending college because of the overwhelming significance of education in industrial advancement.

The occupational perspective of the growing youngster is affected by the location in which he grows up. A rapidly growing area, e.g., Southern California, is likely to present a very different perspective not only of ambitions but of occupations as compared to a stagnant or declining area such as one sees in some parts of New England or the Southern border states. Warner and Abegglen (1955, pp. 69-77) report "productivity ratios" of greater than one (indicating a particular region produces more business leaders than was expected on the basis of population at the time the business leaders were born) in the Middle Atlantic states, New England, the Pacific states, and the East North Central states. Productivity ratios below one were reported for the South — a broad swath from Texas east and including Kentucky, West Virginia, Maryland, and Delaware. Important also are the occupations traditional in a region or in a town.

Education, as a selective force, presents a paradox. On the one hand, it is now the major avenue of entrance to high status occupations and to upward occupational mobility. Warner and Abegglen (1955, pp. 99-114) report that the business leaders they studied were all highly educated men, whatever their level of origin. On the other hand the educational system itself is one of the greatest of all restricting agencies in our society. Its restrictive efforts are manifested in three important ways. First, junior and senior high schools are organized into curricula (general, academic, vocational) which force students to make a selection when very young. Once made, the student has, in effect, rejected a large number of possible occupations to which his chosen curriculum does not lead, and by the time he finds out it is often too late to change. Second, the school is one of the major places in which social class restrictions on occupational choice make themselves apparent. Teachers tend to encourage middle-class children to go on to college, with the result that lower-class children will choose the vocational or general curriculum. Middle-class children therefore get a chance to enter the professions and semiprofessions which require higher education, whereas lower-class children leave high school and find themselves forced to take manual or clerical jobs requiring little education. (Hollingshead, 1949, pp. 168ff.; Lipset, Bendix and Malm, 1955.) Third, the particular school attended affects one's probability of entering certain occupations, especially those of high status. Of course upper class schools, which deliberately prepare the sons of the great to replace their fathers, have always tried to teach not only appropriate knowledge (whether it was Greek and Latin, or music or skills considered proper to a certain style of life, for example, riding, fencing, etc.) but also appropriate attitudes and standards. West (1953) has examined the selectivity of American colleges and found a considerable cleavage between students who supported themselves in college and those who did not. Though the former are very important as a proportion of the increase in college attendance, they tend to enter the more poorly paying professions (education, ministry, or the arts rather than medicine, dentistry, or law). When West restricted her attention to this self-help group alone, she found that college attendance made a definite difference in subsequent earnings, with Ivy League colleges scoring at the top. Clark (1960) has pointed out the manner in which the junior college functions to "cool-out" persons who otherwise would go on to university and fail, at least in the view of the educators at the college.

A final factor which strongly affects one's cultural perspective is social class. Like education, the primary effect of social class restrictions on one's occupational perspective is to narrow one's choice to those one's class knows about, is sympathetic toward, or can help one with. In practice, however, this turns out to be primarily a mobility or aspirational matter rather than one of social selection. In other words, the social class of a person seems to affect the prestige, power, or economic position of the occupation he tries to enter to a greater degree than it affects the particular occupation. Since occupations do differ in prestige, power, and economic position, a net effect here is to shunt lower class persons to semiskilled and personal service occupations and to open the possibility of professional positions to middle class persons. The nature of this process will be commented on further.

The foregoing has dealt with the role of the cultural perspective in occupational social selection. Less attention need be given — because the process is more widely known — to positive restrictions on entry. We refer to the exclusiveness of occupations which wish to regulate the numbers who enter, and to the fact that members of the occupation, being also members of society, reflect in their attitudes towards race, religion, ethnicity, or other occupational stereotypes, whatever the society happens to believe. Various researchers have documented the claim that the school is the bearer of our cultural values. Insofar as teachers are Protestant, white, middle-class, native-born Americans, they tend, so researchers report, to favor children who are like themselves and this preference is manifest in the giving of high marks, in recommendations for honor, scholarships, etc. In addition the middle-class values of such teachers with reference to sex practices, drinking, ambitiousness, etc., may also be reflected in their attitudes toward the child. The importance of these attitudes and their prevalence, however, is very much an open area for further research.

Work Mobility

Research on mobility has tended to revolve about two major questions: How much mobility is there? What are the processes by which persons change their social positions? The answer to the first question helps to give a partial answer to the crucial question of whether class lines in the United States are tightening or not, whereas the answer to the second helps give clues for understanding how the traditional openness of the United States structure can be preserved or increased.

Many studies of amount of mobility have focused on a local community. For reasons of space, we must restrict ourselves to only one — that by Rogoff (1953) — but it is probably the best such study. It occupies such a position because of a technical advance made over other studies; namely, it provides us not simply with a comparison of fathers' occupations with sons' occupations but in addition compares sons' occupations with what one would expect them to be on the basis of probability. In addition, she has performed this operation at two points in time — the period 1905 to 1912 and the period 1938 through the first half of 1941. Her study was carried out in Marion County, Indiana (the city of Indianapolis and a suburban and rural fringe). When Rogoff summarized her measures of occupational mobility she found the mean mobility rate for 1910 to be almost identical with that in 1940, indicating neither less nor more mobility in 1940 than in the earlier period. When she attempted to measure the *direction* of movement using the categories of white collar, blue collar, and farming, and when we divide the ratio she obtained for upward mobility by that for downward mobility, we find the quotient to be .96 for 1910 and 1.20 for 1940. The latter indicates a possible "net" in favor of upward rather than downward mobility, though this seems to be due to a lowering of the amount of downward mobility.

Another kind of study focuses on career mobility rather than intergenerational mobility. Lipset and Bendix's (1952) study of Oakland, California, turned up evidence of an enormous amount of job movement within the career. The 935 heads of working families studied reported 4,530 jobs, or an average of 4.8 jobs each

83

for an average of 25.3 years in the labor force. Those who owned or managed a business were found to be the most heterogeneous in past experience: almost 40 per cent of the shifts into self-employment were from manual jobs, slightly under 30 per cent were from various nonmanual jobs, and only 21.6 per cent were from one form of business ownership to another. Shifts within the occupation were found to be most characteristic of professional, semi-professional, and upper white-collar groups, though skilled workers were also high on this dimension. In spite of this great volume of shifting, however, they found that most of the shifting between groups was with *adjacent* groups, and there was very little permanent shifting between manual and nonmanual occupations. The latter leads Lipset and Bendix (1952) to say "This is perhaps the most fundamental cleavage in American society." (p. 371.) A final important finding is that "upward mobility" has come to mean quite different things for the working class as compared to the middle class. Based on their data, they write, "It is our guess that the creed of individual enterpriser has become by and large a working class preoccupation. Though it may have animated both working class and middle class in the past, it is no longer a middle class ideal today. Instead people in the middle class aspire to become professionals and, as a second choice, upper white-collar workers." (Lipset and Bendix, 1952, p. 504.) Other studies tend to support the picture that Bendix and Lipset give us of the very great amount of occupational movement. (Form and Miller, 1949; Gross, 1959; Reiss, 1955.)

There is evidence that there is a tendency for persons to overemphasize the amount of rigidity in the structure at the present time because of overestimates of the amount of mobility present in the nineteenth century. The labor safety-valve theory has been severely questioned in recent years. That theory held that one reason for the lack of development of social classes in the United States on the model of European social classes was the ability of the Eastern wage earner to "chuck it" if he was not doing well and move out West. In fact, the amount of such movement appears to have been very small. On the whole the data we have would suggest that the opportunity structure apparently has not made it more difficult for persons to change jobs than for their fathers. Class lines do not appear to have tightened but they apparently have not loosened either.

In addition to studies of the amount of mobility, attention has also been given to processes of mobility. Studies have pointed out the role of differential fertility, technological changes, immigration, and political self-government in affecting the manner in which persons move up and down occupationally. Obviously, the individual can rise above his fellows. Just as important, however, are situations in which the group to which the individual belongs changes its relation to other groups in the society. This type of mobility is seen in the rise of social classes, as for example in the replacing of the French feudal lords by the bourgeoisie. It also is present when an important technological change takes place. When a new industry begins, not only are new statuses provided, but also as the importance of the industry increases those who "got in on the ground floor" will rise with the industry. As pointed out in the foregoing, one of the commonest ways an occupation can raise its relative position is to try to make itself into a profession, although some occupations may attempt to do this before they are technically ready for it.

Foote (1953) has claimed that labor as a whole is tending to become professionalized. The indices he calls our attention to are: (1) technology is increasingly the preoccupation of engineers or else it has become automatic; (2) trade unionism is, in one sense, a movement to assure each worker of a career; and (3) there is a growing emphasis on "rules" and general knowledge. Forces such as these together with others such as internal migration within the United States and the increased emphasis on education are likely to affect the number of vacant occupational statuses available in a society but, after all, they are only permissive or facilitating factors. The fact that a position is available does not guarantee that someone will turn up to fill it: *motivation* must be present.

Lipset and Zetterberg (1956) point out the strange paradox exhibited by the United States. The very society that insists that all are equal also continually reassures its young that upward mobility is everyone's right; yet if all are equal, then there are no superior and inferior positions and there is nothing for which to strive. Lipset and Zetterberg (1956) resolve the paradox by pointing out that the very emphasis on equalitarianism makes it necessary to stimulate persons to try to move up, whereas in more rigid societies which freely concede the existence of large class differences, those very differences provide obvious reasons for striving to rise to a higher class. It is in the United States then that motivation to strive upward becomes a problem in the sense that special means must be provided for assuring that persons *will* make efforts to rise. For example, Montague (1954) in a comparative study found that although American boys more generally than British boys accepted mobility as a goal, American boys were actually *more* conscious of social class than the English youth.

There is much evidence of the strength of beliefs in chances for occupational success. Remarkable and more difficult to explain is the persistence of these beliefs in the face of evidence to the contrary and particularly of personal experience to the contrary. Katherine Archibald, (1947) studying a shipyard in Oakland, California, during World War II, found very little of the traditional spirit of individual enterprise. On the contrary, her fellow workers resented authority, especially the front office (whose power, they felt, was not due to merit), and they did not think that education would get a man very far. At the same time they did not reject the belief in the existence of opportunity. They insisted that a man could move up but explained that *they* did not wish to try because the means for doing so were beneath their dignity (bootlicking) or beyond their control (luck). Perhaps the best examination of this phenomenon is by Chinoy (1955) who, confirming the findings of many other researchers, reports that automobile workers had very little ambition as exhibited by the general lack of desire to become foremen in the factories in which they worked. They had definitely not given up, however, nor were they ready to form a working class. They still subscribed to the ideology of success, at least for their children. Further — and this is his most striking finding — Chinoy discovered that *security* itself, while traditionally regarded as the opposite of upward striving and advancement, had become in the worker's mind a type of mobility. Chinoy puts it this way:

> *Questions which were designed to elicit the relative importance assigned to security and opportunities for advance-*

ment frequently proved meaningless; the respondents could see no difference between them. "If you've got security, if you've got something you can fall back on, you're still getting ahead," said a twenty-eight year old truck driver with three children. "If you can put away a couple of hundred dollars so you can take care of any emergency, then you're getting ahead," declared a forty-year old nonskilled maintenance worker with four children. "If you work during a layoff, like back in the depression, that's my idea of working up," commented a thirty-two year old fender wrapper who had been in the plant since 1935. And a thirty-nine year old oiler summed it up: "If you're secure, then you're getting ahead." (Chinoy, 1955, p. 125.)

The strength of such beliefs in the ideology of success is drawn upon also by Lipset and Rogoff (1954) to explain their finding that no significant difference exists between the rates of occupational mobility in America and industrially advanced European countries. The belief that such a difference exists has long been used to explain the lack of a socialist movement or the development of a class conscious proletariat in the United States. Instead, Lipset and Rogoff suggest, the failure of such proletariat to develop must be attributed to the strength of egalitarianism plus the fact of greater economic productivity and a more equal distribution of income and prestige symbols. We referred earlier to the persistence of small business in the United States. Bunzel, (1962) in a study of small business, attributes this persistence in part to the tendency of small businessmen to regard themselves as culture heroes, as guardians of the "agrarian spirit" of the Jeffersonian era and of frontier values. This belief persists in spite of the high mortality of small business and is part of the explanation for the continued strength of motivation to try once again. In the large corporation, the motivation to move in response to opportunity may be facilitated by the corporation itself. Fellin and Likwak (1963) show how bureaucratic jobs involve actual training for change so that mobility is not as disruptive as it might otherwise be.

An important area of research in careers has dealt with the contingencies, which may force radical readjustments, that may occur in the course of a person's lifetime. The shopkeeper may lavish much care in building up a neighborhood following, only suddenly to lose much of his trade to a new supermarket. An important contingency revolves about the aging process, particularly in occupations in sports, piloting for air lines, prostitution, and many types of crime, since many criminals reach the peak of their careers when they are young. In addition, there exist "young men's jobs" and "old men's jobs," a set of beliefs which may or may not be related to actual performance ability as measured by an objective test. Along with this goes a conception of a proper rate of movement related to one's age: one is expected to have passed certain points by a certain age. During the great depression of the 1930's many persons over 40 years of age who had held academic positions were unable to secure jobs in spite of their willingness to accept bottom rank instructorships: an instructorship is a young man's job. Such age grading is particularly likely to be affected by technological changes or rapid expansion. During periods of prosperity when a certain industry is developing rapidly, large numbers of persons may be hired at the same level. They then will rise at about the same rate, although obviously they cannot all be promoted at the same time. Such seems to be the case presently in the electronics industry which large numbers are being encouraged to enter.

Hughes (1960) has pointed to the principle of the point-of-crucial-decision in the career. When does one decide to enter an occupation? The student may decide in high school that he will make physics his lifelong career. He may then proceed in a fairly well-defined pattern throughout high school, college, and graduate work to employment in teaching, research, or on the staff of a factory. We have here a straight career line where the point of crucial decision has been pushed down. The same may be true in medicine where the attempt is made to get persons to secure their fundamental orientation at an early age. Yet such a process, however desirable it may be felt to be for the occupation, obviously places an enormous burden on young people to make long-range decisions at what must necessarily be younger and younger ages. In some of the professions, there is evidence of a recent tendency to reverse this process. Other occupations have very high crucial-decision points. One of these is social work in which persons may decide, in the midst of a different career, to return to school and enter the profession. Most professions resist such late entries, partly because they often are difficult to socialize, and partly because they may be difficult to place in jobs.

In spite of its appeal in current fiction, the bureaucratic career has not been studied intensely. Perhaps the most important conclusion of such research as has been done is that the notion of an undifferentiated set of striving careerists, and the notion of an undifferentiated set of old soldiers waiting out their pensions, are both wrong. There seems, instead, to be a number of distinct types. Presthus (1962) distinguishes among *upward-mobiles* who are strongly oriented to a bureaucratic career and to success in the organization, *indifferents* who make up the uncommitted majority who see their jobs as mere instruments to obtain off-work satisfactions, and *ambivalents* who make up a small, perpetually disturbed minority "who can neither renounce their claims for status and power nor play the disciplined role that would enable them to cash in such claims." (p. 15.)

Moore (1962) describes other internal variations in the large industrial organization. The picture of a "ladder" may be misleading for foremen since they are not likely to advance any further once they have attained the foreman's position. For them, he suggests, the world "platform" may be more apt. There are many different orientations toward organizational success. The "strainer" is not necessarily in the majority or typical. There are also "secure mobiles," who have more modest ambitions. They are not lazy but do not aim as high as the "strainers" do. Some of these may be more aptly conceived of as riding an escalator rather than as climbing a ladder. The main mobile step is made in getting on the escalator. From that point on it would require positive effort to keep from being moved up, albeit slowly. Another kind of career is exhibited by the staff man who must change into the line in order to move very high in the organization, thus adding "diagonal" mobility to "upward" and "downward" mobility. Many persons with engineering degrees regard engineering as little more than a means whereby they may move over into the administrative hierarchy. Moore (1962) suggests that a picture of industrial organizations as being composed of persons in heated competition for the top is, in fact, inaccurate. Only a relatively small proportion desire to move to the top, most being satisfied to stay in their positions and to do their jobs well. In reality industry could not support any large number of persons who desired to move to the top.

Even less attention has been given to downward mobility, especially in the later bureaucratic career. Wilensky and Edwards (1959), describing the career of "skidders" (downward mobile persons) in two large factories, report a continued clinging to the belief in chances for upward mobility. Such a feeling was not anticipatory but retrospective, harking back to better days. The writers confirm the often-reported finding that such persons are politically conservative, particularly the older work life skidders. Martin and Strauss (1956) describe the means organizations use to "cool out" older persons who must be "kicked upstairs," such as creating special positions for them with little authority or responsibility. Good studies of organizational downward mobility have also been made by More (1962) and Whyte (1948, Chapter 11). One concludes that industry, for all of its vaunted emphasis on efficiency and rationality, in fact "carries" a large number of its older persons. This fact may not become known to an industrial organization until automation forces it to re-examine the structure of jobs. It is then that they discover that the work which had been assigned to certain persons can no longer be justified. There actually may have been a long period preceding this in which the work assignment had been adjusted to the man in order to enable him to keep his job, rather than the reverse.

Industry and Personality

The relation between work and personality, although much discussed in impressionistic and global terms, has been the subject of surprisingly little research. Merton's classic description of the bureaucratic personality is not based on systematic research among members of bureaucratic organizations. Davis (1948) found support for the picture Merton presents, but Turner (1947) found a variety of adjustments. He found that the navy disbursing officer may be more concerned with his own bargaining power than with correct application of rules. One would conclude that even in the case of the highly strict task definition one finds in the military, it is not true that one will find only a certain type of personality. Instead the person may adjust the positional requirements to suit his own needs or own definition of the situation. In the case of other industrial positions in which the requirements of the position are not so strict, one might ask whether the position attracts a certain kind of person and then molds him to fit the expectations. There are no real data on this question but one gets certain hints from occupational studies. The assumption by Freud of a direct relation between certain personality traits and occupation (for example, that surgeons were sadists) has never really been studied, and such evidence as we have belies any simple relationship.

Roe (1956) summarizes a great deal of the data on the relation between occupation and personality. From her data, one would conclude that there is indeed a relationship but not a close or neat one. For example, a study of life insurance salesmen by Harrower and Cox (1942) found such salesmen had an interest in people but that this interest was not a personal one. Perhaps this is functional since they could hardly do their jobs if they became personally involved with their clients. In a study of eminent scientists, Roe (1952) relates patterns of personality (rather than traits) to work position, a procedure which seems to be more satisfactory. Scientists' home backgrounds included an emphasis on learning for its own sake rather than for economic and social rewards, and there was a common tendency for them to have been placed on their own resources. Biologists had an orientation which strongly emphasized reliance upon rational controls; physicists were often anxious and neither interested in people nor very good in relating to them in general. The social scientists were deeply concerned about human relations and troubled by them in a way quite foreign to the other two groups. One is never sure, however, whether Roe's findings relate to eminence as such or to eminence in the particular field, or whether they can be generalized to other less eminent scientists.

Henry, (1949) using the Thematic Apperception Test on a sample of over 100 "successful" business executives, sums up his findings as follows: "The value of accumulation and achievement, of self-directedness and independent thought and their rewards in prestige and status and property are found in this group. But they also pay the price of holding these values and of profiting from them. Uncertainty, constant activity, the continual fear of losing ground, the inability to be introspectively leisurely, the ever present fear of failure, and the artificial limitations put upon their emotionalized interpersonal relations — these are some of the costs of this role." (p. 291.) Like Roe's work on scientists, the conclusion is uncertain because of the lack of a control group.

Somewhat better are situational studies, that is, those which examine personality in actual industrial settings. Argyris (1954, a) found that the stereotype of the bank clerk had a basis in reality, at least in the minds of the officers of the bank and those who did the bank's hiring. There was a feeling that one should search for what was called the "right type." The "right type" was a person who was meek, quiet, obedient, tactful, cautious, careful, non-aggressive, submissive, complacent, conservative, and security-conscious. Argyris (1954, a) feels that such a type is functional for the bank because such persons are more willing than others to accept the low salary which bank employees receive, partly because they are not the type who would protest and partly because they value security, which the bank does indeed offer, so highly. The bank apparently attempts to produce such a person. It also rewards those who exemplify this type and punishes those who do not, thus producing a selective process. Here Argyris discovers a paradox. The "right type" is apparently best able to function in positions requiring that he meet with the public, where he must keep his feelings to himself and maintain a studied exterior designed to please the client.

Such was not at all the case among those, such as bookkeepers, who did not meet the public. Argyris (1954, b) claims that bookkeepers had to behave in ways diametrically opposed to the "right type" in order to do their jobs well. They daydreamed a good deal and sang. Such behavior, he claims, is necessary if they are to be able to do their work at all. In addition, the bookkeepers made fewer mistakes when they daydreamed; yet when an officer of a bank came upon such behavior he would tend to punish it as being not in accord with perceptions of the "right type." Consequently, turnover was quite high in the bookkeeping department. The girls in the bookkeeping department therefore found themselves subjected to criticism and censure because of their daydreaming, which led to low morale on their part. At the same time they had to engage in this behavior in order to maintain high efficiency. In this case morale and efficiency are found to be inversely correlated. In a study of hospital nurses, Argyris (1956) found the preferred type to be one who placed high value on the direct provision of health services to the patient and a low value on supervisory activities.

The over-all picture that emerges from Argyris' research is that there exist in organizations conceptions of "desirable" personality types for the organization as a whole, but that such personality types are only functional for certain of the major positions in the organization. The "right type" for the bank thus seems to be functional for tellers and officers but not for bookkeepers, and the "desired" type in the hospital is functional for staff nurses but not for supervisors. Further, insofar as the positional requirements specify a certain kind of personality as desirable for the organization, they incapacitate the organization for handling change. If one emphasizes the nonaggressive bank type, such a bank thus will be in a poor position for aggressive competition with other banks, the increasing trend among banks at present. These data on occupations, scientists, the business executive, the banker, bookkeeper, and hospital nurse together offer more evidence to support the contention that positions select certain kinds of persons rather than that positions mold persons to fit a particular positional requirement. The whole notion of selection, of course, presumes that enough knowledge is available to select the appropriate person and that techniques will enable accurate selection.

On the whole the foregoing evidence does not support the hypothesis that there is a close relationship between personality and work position. The requirements of positions are defined sufficiently loosely to allow for a good deal of diversity of personality. This may be the major reason why Roe did not report a direct relationship between occupation and personality. Wilensky (1956) describes three kinds of positions which union professionals may be asked to fill; "facts and figures," "contact," and "internal communication." He then reports that he found four role-orientations among union professionals: missionaries, professional service, careerist, and "politico." While missionaries tended to be internal communications specialists, professional service persons and careerists to be "facts and figures" men, and while there was a slight tendency for "politicos" to be "contact" men, the striking thing about his data is the lack of perfect correspondence. Approximately the same number of missionaries as are internal communication specialists are also facts and figures and contact men. In addition the number of careerists who are contact men and internal communications specialists exceeds those who are facts and figures men. Such lack of strict correspondence suggests the desirability of flexibility in job description. It also suggests that personality tests can have only a limited usefulness in selection.

CHAPTER 6

WORK GROUPS AND COLLEAGUESHIP

Informal Relations at Work

COLLEAGUES are persons who have a complete involvement in the work situation and feel a sense of responsibility toward one another for the work they perform. Each feels that the other is a full working member of the group. Such persons can be distinguished from those who have only a marginal relationship to the work situation. Among such marginal persons are those whose primary identification is elsewhere, as in the case of women who may be working temporarily in order to help out with family finances or persons who may be restricted to marginal tasks because of race or religion. An upper-class white law firm thus may maintain its reputation for handling only "nice" cases by referring all of the "dirty" or indelicate cases to Negro lawyers who may have no choice but to accept.

What activity is marginal and what is central to the work situation may change over time. Midwifery, nursing, pharmacy, surgery, and optometry once were historic mysteries that existed outside of medicine but have since been brought in as specialities or else as subordinate to medical persons. (Wardwell, 1963.) Sometimes, however, persons who occupy marginal positions may come to influence the central colleague very much. The accountant is brought in to do a specific job but may nevertheless have great influence on the workings of an organization. Similarly, lawyers, scientists, and other professionals may be desired and required. One wishes more than mere competence or skill from such persons; one also wants their sympathy and understanding. Their loyalty is often difficult to secure, however, since they are not full colleagues in the organization but retain outside loyalties.

Considerable research has been done on the problem of building colleagueship and several distinct means have been pointed to and described. Perhaps the most important is control of the entry of new members to the occupation or the organization. One can see the problem illustrated in occupations such as harvest work where there is a large reservoir population composed of women, youngsters, and minority group members who are available when they are needed. Professional harvest workers are likely to resist the entry of those persons since they depress wages and have only a minimal interest in working conditions and long-range problems faced by the industry. A second means for developing colleagueship is to attempt deliberately to develop a consciousness of occupation. For this purpose leaders in the occupation may develop a public relations image of the occupation as one dedicated to public service. Riley (1963) has described the way in which corporations attempt to develop such an image for themselves. In order to develop such an occupational consciousness it becomes essential that the members of the occupation learn to value their activities highly; this is one of the objects of the training process. The high evaluation furthermore is not restricted to persons in occupations that have high prestige. A common statement from persons who act as aids to others, such as technicians, assistants, nurses, and the like, therefore is that they save their masters from their own mistakes.

Another way of developing a high sense of the importance of one's own occupation is to develop a sense of superiority over other occupations and over the clients with whom one deals. Lipset, Trow, and Coleman (1956) in a study of the International Typographical Union advance what they call the "marginal status hypothesis." Printers regard themselves as the elite group among the manual workers. They have always had to be literate, are better educated and tend to have a stronger middle-class orientation than do other manual workers. Consequently one could predict that they would prefer to associate with middle-class persons, but if that were not possible they would be found to be associating with other printers. Such was the finding of the research. Colleagueship can be developed by deliberately encouraging informal association among colleagues. Lipset, Trow, and Coleman thus describe the "occupational community" of the printers which takes the form of many clubs and a good deal of informal visiting with one another. Persons most active in the occupational community were also found to be those most involved in and informed about union and political affairs. Another factor that developed informal contacts among the printers was night work which broke up the usual pattern of family and recreational life and threw the printers together for long periods. A final factor that contributes to a sense of colleagueship is the development of various norms or rules of the game to control competition among members and hence limit competition between the occupation and other occupations. Many examples are available but perhaps the outstanding ones are the "ethics" of professional groups.

When means such as these are employed to develop a strong sense of attachment and a strong sense of obligation to one's occupation or organization, the question may be raised: About what actions do a man's colleagues have the right to be concerned? Wherein lie his areas of privacy? Colleagues are likely to assume that they have a right to be concerned about any actions which may affect the welfare of the work organization. As a consequence, every occupation and every well-developed organization will try to develop a set of expectations or obligations towards one another among its members. One of the most important of such obligations is the obligation of secrecy. We do not refer only to keeping the client's affairs secret but also to the obligation to double talk, that is, to talk in one frame of reference to one's clients or society at large and a different frame of reference to one's colleagues. This is not simply a matter of "fooling the client" for if the engineer were to tell the line manager the plain truth in technical language, he would tell him very little or simply alarm him. Consequently he tells him in language that he will understand. It is the professional here who faces the most difficulty perhaps, since much of what he must deal with on an everyday routine basis consists of matters which are crises to other people. His language therefore must enable him to discuss objectively the affairs of his client and if his client hears of such objectivity it may sound to him as though the professional were being very impersonal and callous towards him. It is only through such a language, however, that professionals may be enabled to perform at all.

One wishes colleagues who are more than technically competent: one wants persons with whom one feels he can communicate and who can be counted on to understand. That too is part of the reason why colleagues will develop a special language or argot to communicate with one another. Such a language also may tell one a good deal about how the occupation regards itself. Elkin (1946) thus points out that the language of the soldier is related to his image of solidarity (G.I.); to his freedom from customary social restraints (the omnipresent obscene adjectives); belief in his strength ("sweat out"); and his attitude towards authority ("chicken"). Once such an argot is fully developed it not only identifies colleagues and facilitates communication among them, but also symbolizes the strength of ties between them. In addition it provides one with an infallible way of recognizing the competent and experienced since only they will be able to use the language with facility.

One of the major subjects of research in industrial relations from the beginning was the informal work group. To many workers these groups seem hardly worth noting since they seem to be so natural as to be taken for granted. On the other hand, management often regards them with great suspicion, feeling that they are not only a waste of time but centers in which troublemakers may get a hearing. The persistence and universality of these groups suggest however that they must perform important functions for their members and research implies that they do.

There are four functions of informal groups. *One,* they provide protection and assistance to members. Because members of such groups feel at one with one another, they will take over one another's work when necessary, will make excuses to management for one another, and support their members if one is attacked. *Two,* informal groups have communication functions. These often are made up of men or women from different parts of the organization. A group composed of persons who belong to different departments therefore will communicate to one another what is going on in the various departments and it becomes possible to prepare for forthcoming changes. This, of course, is the often-referred to "grapevine." A good study of the relation between social structure and informal communication was carried out at a summer camp by Larsen and Hill (1958). *Three,* informal groups control their members' behavior. They teach them proper behavior and apply sanctions when members deviate. They thus are one of the major "educational facilities" in organizations in which persons are taught the facts of organizational life. *Four,* informal groups provide personal satisfactions. Since the members trust each other they provide an opportunity in which persons can relax and "let down their hair" in one another's presence. Here one finds persons who understand, who are interested in one's problems; this is extremely important in work situations where the work is critical or where failure may be particularly serious.

In the professions this is particularly likely to be the case. In medicine, for example, no matter how skilled the physician is, some of his patients are going to die. In religion, no matter how the clergyman may war against the devil, the devil is going to win in the case of some of his charges. In teaching, no matter how skilled the teacher is, some of the members of the class are going to fail. In industrial organizations, no matter how skilled an engineer may be, a process run may fail and cost the company a large amount of money. It is the informal work group that comes in in such times to give the individual a sense of assurance so that he will not crack up in the face of such failure. Here is the only group before which it is safe to recount mistakes and which can in turn tell him of similar mistakes and thus enable him to regain his faith in himself. The presence of such a colleague group is an intimate part of the whole phenomenon of self-confidence. A major reason why the new teacher, lawyer, counselor, or executive may feel anxiety and self-doubt is not simply that he lacks experience. He also will feel this way because new persons are not admitted to colleague groups until the other members feel that they can trust them. Until then they must suffer the doubt and uncertainties about their own abilities alone.

99

Although much research has been conducted on such informal groups their obvious importance has led to an overemphasis on them and their significance. Mayo and Lombard (1944), in the early period of research on such groups, went so far as to claim that high turnover in the aircraft plants in California during World War II was due largely to the lack of such friendship groups, in turn due to high mobility among the workers. As researchers began to study the data, however, it began to be clear that a great many workers did not belong to such groups. One obvious exception were "rate-busters" who deliberately rejected group standards and worked at their top capacity. A study of British longshoremen reported that many persons deliberately avoided such groups because they wished to shun personal involvement in work gangs. (*The Dock Worker*, 1954, pp. 66ff.)

More recent research does not support the claim that is sometimes made that the more cohesive a group the higher its productivity. Seashore (1954), after a careful study, concluded that high cohesiveness would have the effect of *narrowing* the range of the individual outputs in a group so that persons would tend to produce at about the same rate, but that the rate of output might be high or low depending on whether or not persons were oriented toward management goals. Many persons feel it to be plausible that more satisfied workers should work harder. Homans (1961, p. 282) after a survey of data on this question, concludes that whether or not the two are related depends on the frequency with which the activity is rewarded. Often the more satisfied a man is the *less* he wants to do and the less productive he is precisely because he is satisfied.

Other kinds of research have attempted to account for the formation of such groups and their effects on work methods. James (1951), Mack (1954), and Sayles (1958) have shown their formation to be related to the layout of the physical work facilities themselves. Sayles (1958, Chapter 3) found the following factors to be important in explaining the presence of such groups: relative position on the promotional ladder of the plant; relative size and importance of the group (with the more solidary groups often being the larger rather than the smaller ones); similarity of jobs; essentiality of the work; and the precision with which management was

100

able to measure work load and pace. Informal organizations may lead to work methods changes, as when workers exchange jobs or when a worker takes over a colleague's job to enable him to take a rest. Gross (1953) found that informal occasions were used by supervisors to size up the job abilities of their subordinates.

Sayles (1958) has suggested that the study of the friendship clique has limited attention to the stabilizing functions of small groups. He draws attention to another type of group, characterized as an *interest group*. Instead of protecting the status quo, holding tight to work standards, resisting rule enforcement and the like, interest groups seek to *improve* the relative position of the members of the group. Improvements can take the form of looser standards, better seniority, more overtime, better supervision, better equipment, and the like.

Sayles develops a typology of such work groups which relates to their participation in the grievance process. (1) *Apathetic* groups were the least likely to develop grievances or engage in concerted action to pressure management and the union, although they were not ranked highest by management for productivity or cooperativeness. Leadership was dispersed among the members with relatively little cohesiveness. (2) *Erratic* groups exhibited no relation between the seriousness of their grievances and the intensity of their protests. Issues that both management and the union considered minor and which could be settled by brief discussions would suddenly erupt into major grievances. At the same time deep-seated grievances might exist for a long time with no apparent reaction. Management regarded this type of a group as very dangerous because they were unpredictable. Such groups had highly autocratic leadership who might just as easily be converted into favorable relationships with management as to any other kind of relationship. (3) *Strategic* groups were shrewdly calculating pressure groups who demanded constant attention to their problems and had the ability to back up their demands by group action. These were highly cohesive with a leadership consisting of a small corps of highly active and influential group members. They made up the heart of the union as well as the grievance activity in their respective plants. The men had what were considered good jobs (though not the best) in the plant and maintained good production records over the long run in many such groups, though not necessarily in all of them. (4) *Conservative* groups were the least likely to use concerted action without warning (as well as less likely to participate in union affairs). The strength of these groups was insured by their possessing a monopoly of critical scarce skills. They were self-oriented groups interested in improving their position in the work organizations. They would not engage in unpredictable walkouts but a quick stoppage was always a possibility. Aware of their latent strength they did not demand the immediate service that the Erratic or Strategic groups did.

Sayles (1958) found a close relationship between the type of work that was done and the likelihood of membership in one of these four types. What is distinctive in such a classification is that these groups are seen to be "free enterprise units" attempting to increase their share of the goods and favors which the organization has to offer. They are self-oriented, even turning against fellow workers if it will suit their group better. They are not limited to those in direct day-to-day interaction with each other but may contain a hundred or more workers who share common objectives. The result may be not a system tending toward equilibrium but rather an increasing instability as groups continue to battle for what they think they deserve.

Professionals in Industry °

Much of the research on the professions in sociology has used the model of the free (self-employed) professional. As far back as 100 years ago, however, there were only about one-half as many free professionals as there were salaried professionals, whereas, as already pointed out, in many "old" professions such as teaching and the ministry, independent practice has never been the norm. The trend has continued. Randle (1959, p. 128) shows that in the twelve-year period after World War II, when the number of production workers increased by 6 per cent in the United States, the

---

°Portions of the following discussion are drawn from Edward Gross, "Industrial Relations," in R. E. L. Faris, *Handbook of Modern Sociology*, Chicago: Rand McNally, 1964, Chap. 17. The writer is grateful to the publisher for permission to do so.

number of scientists and engineers in industry increased four-fold. The increase in the proportion of salaried professionals is due in part to the demand for wholly new services, particularly research and development, and in part to the increased hiring by organizations of members of "old" professions (lawyers, physicians) as staff members.

Professional and bureaucratic orientations to work have much in common. (Blau and Scott, 1962, pp. 60-62.) Both emphasize universalistic standards, specificity of function, affective neutrality, and evaluation of competence on the basis of performance rather than ascribed characteristics such as sex or birth order. In at least two basic respects, however, the professional and the bureaucratic orientation clash. The bureaucratic orientation, as expressed in the modern business corporation, is directed towards the increase in the self-interest of the corporation. The professional is expected to be oriented towards service towards his client. This does not mean that the professional is expected to be uninterested in improving his own position; rather, the relations in the profession are so structured that only by serving his client does he serve himself. The professional in the organization will be expected to regard the organization as his "client." At the same time, since he may be involved in product research or in activities which relate the firm to the outside world, he will be equally interested in serving the public at large as an outside client, an orientation which may run afoul of the organization's desire to have him serve the organization only. A second important contrast is in the structure of authority. In the organization, decision-making is hierarchically organized; in the profession colleague control is decisive. Kornhauser (1962) has summarized the major issues as conflicts in the attainment of goals, conflicts over controls, conflicts over incentives and over influence in industry. Whether he is in an organization or not, the scientist will seek to carry on research and make contributions to knowledge. In industrial organizations he will find himself strongly pressured to orient his research to "practical" concerns or to those that may have some possible future use to the organization. At the same time there is a continuing dilemma, for organizations are repeatedly confronted with "useless" types of research which have later turned out to be enormously profitable. Putting one's money on research activities means, however, taking long-range risks.

The major conflict occurs over the difference between bureaucratic authority and colleague (or professional) authority. Kornhauser (1962, Chapter III) sees these problems of control becoming crystallized about the issues of recruitment, organization, supervision, and communication. The problem of the loyalty of the professional — whether to one's professional colleagues or to the organization that employs one — has long been recognized although only recently has any research been directed to it. Reissman (1949) used the term "functional bureaucrat" to refer to the type of bureaucrat who is oriented towards his professional group rather than to the bureaucracy itself. Wilensky (1956, pp. 129-144) similarly found that the "professional service" labor union intellectual was oriented to his colleagues outside the union, and might even be induced to go to work for company management. Caplow and McGee (1958, p. 85) described the scholar's orientation to his institution as sometimes operating to disorient him from his discipline. Professionally-oriented scholars may regard their institution as "a temporary shelter" where they can continue to pursue their careers.

These orientations have been intensely studied by Gouldner (1957-58) in a small private liberal arts college with results which likely are generalizable to industrial organizations. Using the three criteria of loyalty to the employing organization, commitment to specialized role skills, and reference group orientation, he draws a distinction between "cosmopolitans" and "locals." "Cosmopolitans" (in contrast to locals) have a strong outer reference group orientation and a high commitment to specialized role skills but low loyalty to the employee organization. Factor analysis reveals certain clusters. The "locals" were found to be divisible into the "dedicated" (who support organization values), the "true bureaucrats" (who support the security of the organization against outside criticism and who tend to be oriented to the local community), the "home-guard" (mostly middle administration persons who got their degrees at that college and now are back), the "elders" (old-timers who know many people and who have a strong peer group reference). "Cosmopolitans" were of two types: the "out-

siders" (who are in but not of the university) and "empire-build-
ers" (who have a departmental orientation). The "locals" as a
whole are characterized by loyalty and the "cosmopolitans" as a
whole by emphasis on expertise. Blau and Scott (1962) suggest a
modification of the Gouldner conclusions because of contradictory
findings reported by Bennis, *et al.* (1958) in a study of nurses.
They suggest that "commitment to professional skills will be associated with low organization loyalty only if professional opportunities are more limited in the organization under consideration
than in others with which it competes for manpower." (p. 71.)

The conflict over professional incentives arises from the fact
that the scientific professions judge a man by his contributions
through research papers, attendance at professional meetings and
the like, whereas the employing organization evaluates a man on
the basis of his contributions to production and sales or to new or
improved devices, and rewards the man through promotions, income and increased power. Many firms are attempting to utilize
professional incentives by giving their scientists and other professionals time off to attend professional meetings, paying their professional dues, giving them tuition refunds for further professional
training, allowing publication of research results under certain
conditions, and providing double ladders of advancement so that
a man can remain a scientist yet still get ahead in the company.

Four kinds of professional organizations can be distinguished —
the learned society, the professional association, the trade union,
and the professional union. Only the last three are of importance
for the professional in organizations. Professional associations are
oriented to the improvement of the welfare of their members. As
such they usually include members of management as well as scientists and others who are not involved in administrative activities.
Trade unions such as the American Federation of Technical Engineers (AFL-CIO) attempt to follow the model of the standard trade
union in emphasizing the special advantages of trade union membership and bringing pressure to bear on members of management
to improve the lot of engineers, architects, chemists, bateriologists,
and other professional employees. Membership often is open to
technicians and engineers who perform no research or scientific
functions but is closed to those in managerial positions.

The professional union as exemplified by the one-time national union, the Engineers and Scientists of America, is something of a hybrid organization. It stresses the special needs of professionals at the same time giving direct attention to the employee status of its members and engages in collective bargaining. By and large the collective bargaining principle has not made spectacular gains among engineers and scientists. Within recent years it may actually have declined in the face of increasing influence of professional associations. As such one finds a typical meeting of industrial professionals including both members of management and staffs who work under them. Special problems in the development of solidarity are therefore presented, particuarly since one of the main problems, as we have pointed out, is the conflict over authority. (Strauss, 1964.)

CHAPTER 7

LABOR UNIONS

Labor as a Social Movement: Ideologies and Trends

AVERAGE annual membership in American labor unions has fluctuated over the years, exhibiting many ups and downs. For example, from a membership of more than five million in 1920, it dropped to less than three million in 1933 but rose to eight and one-half million in 1940. Since then, unions have made spectacular gains and at present about one-third of organizable (mainly non-agricultural) workers are members of unions. They tend to be a lower middle socioeconomic status group, heavily concentrated in cities and in certain industries, especially manufacturing, mining, transportation and communication, entertainment and construction. The workers covered by collective bargaining agreements are around 70 per cent for manufacturing and over 90 per cent in certain kinds of manufacturing such as automobiles, basic steel, trucking, and railroading. On the other hand the figures are very low for farming, domestic service, and many branches of trade. Only one-sixth of white-collar workers are unionized, though the proportion exhibits wide variations in different cities.

Although the total number of union members has continued to increase, at least since World War II, the proportion organized has not gone up appreciably. Bernstein (1954, a; 1954, b), surveying labor unions since the latter part of the nineteenth century, concludes that they have tended to exhibit a spasmodic growth, being particularly affected by periods of social unrest and by cataclysms such as wars. He speculates that for the future the number of labor union members will continue to grow at a steady rate but may suddenly spurt up should there be another period of social unrest or upheaval.

Bell (1960) strongly disputes this conclusion. Labor organization in the United States has proceeded by what he calls "eruption, extension and enforcement." "Eruption" refers to a great surge in membership, as exhibited during the late thirties in the United States. Extension takes place when, after a breakthrough, comparable firms are forced into line. Enforcement takes place through such devices as closed shops, union shops, and other legal means for blanketing workers into union membership. Enforcement has been the typical pattern in the AFL building trades, and other unions such as the railroad unions may enlarge their membership in the future in the same way. Bell's conclusion is that future growth will occur mainly through extension and enforcement, for the most part the latter. He sees no likelihood of eruption, at least in the near future, because of the following considerations.

In manufacturing (with the exception of textiles and chemicals) and in mining and rail transport, most industry is almost completely organized. The big business firms in the economy are in the main unionized. A *Fortune* survey of a 102 (out of 150) manufacturing firms employing more than 10,000 workers showed that 55 were between 80 to 100 per cent organized and another 30 between 50 to 80 per cent organized. (Bell, 1960, p. 91.) The unorganized segments are almost completely supervisory and white-collar workers and there does not seem any great likelihood of unionizing them in the immediate future. The remaining unorganized areas in manufacturing are largely small-sized firms which are both difficult to get to and difficult to organize. Many are in small towns in the South where, because of the dependence of the town on the industry, the political response to unionists is likely to be very hostile. In trade and service small units also tend to predominate. In addition management has become far more generous, in part because of union pressures, in providing many fringes and benefits the absence of which were once one of the unions' strongest talking points. In the past government provided enforcement but Bell sees less likelihood of such enforcement in the future. For one thing government is no longer as favorable to unions as it was during the period that led to the passage of the Wagner Act.

Ways (1963) refers to the increasing irritation of the general public with strikes, and the feeling that such strikes hurt the country in the fighting of the cold war. Still another problem has been the desertion of the labor union movement by the liberal intellectuals in part because of the intellectuals' increasing identification with national goals and in part because of a loss of patience with unions concerning what are felt to be their "narrow" interests in their own self-advancement and growth of strength. Yet, Ways (1963) points out, any conclusion that labor in the United States will henceforth become weak or that it is suffering from a "failure of nerve" is not tenable. The four largest labor unions, the Teamsters, Steelworkers, United Automobile Workers, and Machinists, which together account for one-quarter of all organized workers, are exceedingly lively unions at present. Unions are not growing as rapidly as they once did because of powerful forces which were not present earlier. The unions have not gone backwards in numbers or in proportion organized in spite of the struggles in some of them over Communism, the effects of the Taft-Hartley Law, and the McClellan investigations. They have also managed to hold their own in spite of the fact that the proportion of production workers has been declining in proportion to the total work force, and that an increasing proportion of the work force is white-collar.

On the question of the motives for union affiliation, no simple answer can be given. Some have sought an answer in general terms. For example Bakke (1946) thinks the question must be answered in terms of a theory of motivation in which particular wants are explained in terms of broader needs or goals such as creature sufficiency, control over one's own affairs, integrity, and understanding. Ellsworth (1952) used this approach in an analysis of a manufacturing company and found it necessary to add security and satisfactory working conditions as needs. Others have sought for a general answer by inquiring into factors associated with unionization. Commons (1910) advanced the theory that unions arose in the United States when expanding markets forced a difference of interests on employers and journeymen. Perlman (1949) laid emphasis on the desire of the worker for a type of job proprietorship or security. Tannenbaum (1947; 1951) directs attention to the attempt to regain the values of fellowship, dignity and a sense of personal worth which he feels were destroyed by the growth of large-scale industry.

Such theories have drawn heavily on analyses of the history of labor organization in the United States. Often those who survey that history characterize the goals of union members in terms of the cleavage between those who see the labor union as the means toward ideological ends and those who see it as the means towards instrumental goals. Certainly United States labor history shows elements of both. There were powerful groups desiring the wholesale reconstruction of society such as the Knights of Labor and the International Workers of the World. The occurrence of bloody combats such as the Haymarket Riot of 1886 and the Homestead Strike of 1892 suggests that management and the general public were far from willing to grant labor unions the right to bargain collectively. The first major accusation of Communist backing was directed at the leaders of the steel strike of 1919 and that factor, together with labor's failure to organize the mass production industries and the pressures of both prosperity and depression, dealt labor organization a blow from which it did not recover until 1935. The passage of the Wagner Act in that year signaled an important change in labor union tactics for it was shown how valuable a weapon legislation might be when used to support labor demands and it helped labor throw off the reputation it had with many for being radical.

Present-day labor union ideology has tended to follow the direction given it long ago by Samuel Gompers who helped turn it away from revolutionary objectives to the pursuit of limited goals within the context of capitalism. The major form that radicalism now takes among labor unions is the infiltration of some labor unions by Communists. In general, labor union members do not look to their unions to change the basic structure of American society. Differences between the unions at present are likely to be organizational and tactical rather than ideological. Caplow (1954, pp. 195-198) characterizes the distinction between the AFL and CIO (before they merged) by describing the former as restrictive and the latter as expansive. The former tried to maintain a monopoly or near monopoly of a service by controlling entry into the occupation. The latter, composed of semiskilled and unskilled workers and recognizing that it could not control entry, tried to control the labor market by encouraging minority groups, women and those who would otherwise form a reservoir labor supply to join the union. In turn the inability of the expansive type of union to control its policies from within has led it into active involvement in state and national politics to secure favorable legislation. Of course, when whole industries which affect the national welfare are involved it is difficult to keep state and federal governments from entering into labor relations.

The white-collar unions seem to represent a tendency closer to the model of the CIO than to that of the AFL. Mills has characterized their unionism, like that of wage-workers, as "expedient and instrumental, rather than principled or ideological." (Mills, 1951, p. 316.) When white-collar workers go union they seem to do so mainly from a desire for the economic benefits the union can supply rather than from an identification with the labor movement or with a political point of view. The CIO was better set up to handle such narrow interests and in any case the white-collar group is highly heterogeneous, with entry very difficult to control.

A number of researchers have gone to industries and asked samples of workers what they want from their unions. Rose (1952), in a study of a Teamsters' local in St. Louis, Missouri, found that the workers felt the main function of their union was the betterment of wages and working conditions, but there was a strong interest in other matters such as health benefits and security. While he found little evidence of a "class struggle mentality," Rose reports there was strong support of the policy of using union funds for political activity. Purcell's (1953) packing house workers gave as their most important reason for union allegiance the "job protection and status" that the union offered; "decent wages" took second place as a motive for union membership. Rosen and Rosen (1955) report that only about one-half of the members of District #9, International Association of Machinists, who were sampled supported the union policy of taking an active part in politics.

111

Like Rose's subjects, however, the machinists strongly favored union support of political candidates who backed pro-labor legislation.

Another important finding of the Rosens was the strong desire of the machinists to be kept informed of what the union leadership was doing, not only at the local level but also at the district level. Sayles and Strauss (1953) found that almost every person they interviewed in their sample of a number of union locals felt strongly that the union was necessary for economic security and protection against arbitrary management action. Walker and Guest (1952, b) found that union membership in an automobile assembly plant gave the worker a feeling of personal identity and belonging which neither work group relations nor relations with management supplied.

Long ago Hoxie (1917) distinguished five main functional types of unionism: business unionism (where the union accepts the wage system and seeks the best terms of employment through collective bargaining); uplift or friendly unionism (which accepts the wage system, stresses mutual insurance, cooperation and general social amelioration); revolutionary unionism (which rejects the wage system and aims to overthrow the social order with either a socialistic or an anarchistic approach, the former aiming to set up a socialist state, the latter to use sabotage and other forms of direct action); predatory unionism (which has no particular philosophy but aims at the self-interest of its membership either through open bargaining and secret bribery and violence or through guerilla unionism against the employer); and dependent unionism (which relies either on support of others outside their own group or company support as in the case of company unions). The present-day American union movement can be described as strongly favoring business unionism but with some uplift or friendly unionism and occasional predatory unionism.

The Union in the Work Plant

When a union enters a work plant it produces profound changes in the communication structure. The grievance, as a new formal means of communication, becomes significant. When a worker has a complaint he normally carries it to his foreman who usually will try to deal with it on the spot. Only as a last result will he carry it further up. The same is true of his superior in turn, should the grievance come to his attention. A union can carry grievances to any level it chooses. If the union steward is concerned about the issue it may even be carried immediately to the very top. The result may be great pressure on the first-level supervisor to respond to the grievance or try to anticipate it before it is taken up.

The entry of the union also means the presence of union representatives in all shops of the industrial organization. These men often have privileged status. They may enjoy top seniority, have relatively high wages, and have the right to leave their jobs to take care of union business. Individually stewards and committeemen do not have much power but they possess the authority to call into action the resources of a national labor union, which may be richer and more powerful than the owners and managers in any particular concern. The need to meet management on equal terms has led national unions to add to their staffs experts in law, race relations, economics, public relations, housing, insurance, and many other areas. Management will not lightly take up arms against such an organization. Whyte (1961, pp. 501-503) has suggested that the pressures of union demands and the increased use of professionals by unions has led management to expand its own personnel functions a great deal, as it has found it necessary to justify its actions and to keep careful records to provide evidence for claims it may make.

When a union enters an organization for the first time management occasionally rejects it, regarding it as temporary. More commonly management accepts the union but attempts to conduct business as if the union were not there. It may, for example, continue to hire and fire employees without checking with the union or even considering whether this may be a proper subject for union-management negotiations. This process is often facilitated by the use of vague language in the union contract. Such language is a reflection of the fact that union-management relations are power relations and the contract represents what is in many cases the terms of a truce. Third, management may indeed recognize that the presence of the union means a genuine change in the social structure of the organization but it may attempt to anticipate union demands by freely making offers, assuming that such gifts will be appreciated by the union. The union will desire that management always check with it so that the union's position with reference to its membership is not threatened. Of importance also is the effect of a union contract on the lower supervisors. They usually have not been consulted in the process of negotiation and may feel that top management is not sincere in its contractual promises. The result will be continued conflicts at the lower levels.

Sayles and Strauss (1953, Chapter 4), call attention to the extent to which the grievance process has eroded the power of the foreman. Theoretically, the steward is the first man to whom a worker turns with a grievance. Increasingly the steward is bypassed by both worker and the steward's own superiors in the union structure. The worker does not go to the steward but to whomever he thinks can get him what he wants — often someone much higher in the union organization. This man — perhaps a committeeman or union officer — goes directly to the head of the personnel department or plant manager, a decision is made, and the foreman is ordered to take care of the problem. Even if a worker goes to his steward, the latter, recognizing he has little power and knowledge and perhaps reluctant to do battle with a man who may be his foreman, passes the grievance right on up to someone higher in the union hierarchy. Hence both foreman and steward may come to play minor roles in the grievance process. As both foreman and steward withdraw from the bargaining process, the tendency to push issues further up is accentuated.

Worker Involvement in Labor Unions

The growth of unions in the United States has created a new channel of upward mobility for some, new men of power, and a new status. For a few, especially in certain industries such as garment making, membership in the union is of supreme importance, giving their behavior meaning and their lives a purpose. Data on rank and file attitudes indicate, however, that such strong involvement is rare. Miller and Young (1955), in a study of six union locals in Columbus, Ohio, characterized the feelings of most workers as "disinterested allegiance." Sayles and Strauss (1953, pp. 224-225) found that while their sample strongly accepted the economic function of their unions, only a minority showed emotional identification with the union's organizational goals. The apparent apathy of union members toward internal union activities has been noted by many. Schneider (1957, pp. 265-267) offers a number of possible reasons: wages and such "practical" matters are not "burning issues," workers feel they have little control over their unions, and perhaps some are resisting oppressive control by the union.

Sayles and Strauss (1953, pp. 225-230), making use of projective techniques, report that workers express a feeling of shame at having to accept union help in attaining their goals, doubts about attacking the company, and fear of management reprisal. Others have raised the question of whether the lack of "emotional identification" is a problem, for it is certainly not the only measure of loyalty or participation. Kovner and Lahne (1953) point out the importance of not ignoring the great amount of union talk that takes place in the shop and the fact that many questions are settled at the shop level by the union steward. Rose (1952, pp. 46-54) found a good deal of participation in Teamsters local 688, if one included in participation not only attendance at union meetings but also support of the union during periods of contract negotiation, reading and understanding the union contract, and serving on picket lines. Sayles and Strauss (1953, p. 223), while noting that participation is not high when it has to do with collective bargaining only, nevertheless are careful to point out that it may reach great heights when workers are asked to serve on the picket line.

These data strongly suggest that union members are selective in their participation, and apparently do not support any and all union activities. Rosen and Rosen (1955, pp. 66-69) found that the machinists they studied could be divided into four groups: the "Pickers and Choosers," who selectively decide on their area of satisfaction and dissatisfaction and do not generalize from one issue to all others; "Patriots" who seem to be satisfied with almost anything the union does; "Gripers" who answer "dissatisfied" to all questions about union activities; and "Fence-sitters" who are undecided. ("Pickers and Choosers" included most workers, with "Patriots" in second place.) Form and Dansereau (1957), in a study of a United

Automobile Workers local, found they could classify workers according to their orientations toward union functions and that participation reflected those orientations. Persons with "social" orientations (who viewed the union as fraternal and social) have the highest participation rates, those with "economic" orientations are second, while those with "political" orientations see the union merely as a device to protect them from arbitrary management rules. Whether such participation is relevant to loyalty to the union in time of crisis or is correlated with other types of participation (such as attempts to control the union leadership) are clearly the most important questions. Correlates of participation have been carefully examined by Tannenbaum and Kahn (1958).

This raises the general question of democracy and bureaucracy in the government of trade unions. Whether or not unions should be democratically organized has become a serious question particularly in the English-speaking democracies. Those who argue that unions are public institutions claim that their structure should be democratic. Others, seeing unions as voluntary associations acting for their members, claim that their internal structure is the business of the membership only. Coleman (1956) points to pressures from management, government, and members on union leadership to maintain a democratic organization. Members exert pressure on their leaders because of the democratic values of the members and because often the union arose as an expression of opposition to autocratic practices and remains a symbol of opposition to such practices. Bureaucratic decision-making can, however, go on within the framework of what is little more than lip-service to democratic processes by keeping the members busy in extracurricular activities which gives them a "sense" of participation, by contrasting the behavior of the union leaders with the claimed autocratic behavior of management at some distant time in the past, and, of course, by referring to opponents as pro-Communist or pro-company.

Lipset (1960) advances a number of hypotheses which predict the degree of democratic control in labor unions. The need for bureaucracy increases as a labor union grows large and a system of rational administration becomes necessary. In addition, the need to deal effectively with a centralized industrial organization, as in the case of the Steelworkers, requires that the union should set up a centralized structure. There is a major dilemma in the democratic organization of labor unions. Management criticizes labor union leaders for running their unions with no control from the membership, citing the poor attendance at union meetings as proof of tight control. At the same time management desires "responsibility": when the union leader speaks, he should be able to deliver, and prevent quickie or wildcat strikes. Yet the latter often may be a reflection of membership opposition, the absence of which management was earlier deploring. The endeavor to provide such "responsibility" obviously increases the permanency of tenure of the office holders in the union.

In highly competitive industries, such as the garment trades, the union may press the industry to become more bureaucratized so that the union can deal with it more easily. The same thing happens because government boards in collective bargaining find it easier to deal with a single international body or even a federation than with many local units. As such control over decisions shifts farther and farther away from local levels, there is consequent decline in membership participation and interest in local affairs. Another factor increasing the hold of the bureaucracy over the labor union is its monopoly of the means of communication, such monopoly being reduced should there exist alternative sources of information like the Yiddish Press in the early days of the garment unions or the Catholic press in the case of Catholic workers. The tenure of union leaders is further insured by their monopoly of political skills since most workers have no opportunity to give speeches or become proficient in the skills necessary to attain union leadership. Evidence in support of this claim comes from the situation in Actors' Equity wherein members are persons whose jobs require them to appear before audiences and deliver speeches. They would be expected to feel more at ease in participating actively in union affairs, and, in fact, do. The status of union leaders themselves is important.

Mills (1948) has seen in the labor union movement a new avenue of upward mobility for workers; certainly some have risen to positions of great prestige and power in unions. The union offers, furthermore, very real advantages to the worker. Union stewards are often the last to be laid off and the first to be rehired. They

117

are permitted to take time off from their work to handle union affairs, and the higher up in the union a man is the more time may he be allowed. Although there are various types of motivation evident in the union leader — Mills suggesting three types, the "business-like" man, the "political" man, and the "disgruntled working" man, (Chinoy [1955, pp. 104-105] adds a fourth, namely those pushed into union activity by friends) — for "political" and "business-like" men in particular the union represents a very important opportunity. In political life on the outside, the defeated incumbent of public office may return to private life often without serious loss of income or prestige. Such is not the case in labor unions. A man who has been defeated for a union office may find it impossible to drop back to the lowly status of worker in his shop. This provides a pressure on leaders to maintain their control over the membership. Supporting evidence comes from Actors' Equity and the American Newspaper Guild in which the difference in status between members and the leadership is very slight if it exists at all and in which persons hence are not reluctant to return to a nonbureaucratic status. A similar situation is present in the International Typographical Union. After discussing other factors, however, Lipset is careful to point out that the lack of democratic organization within labor unions does not necessarily mean that labor unions have an undemocratic effect on the society as a whole. Quite the contrary, the security of tenure of the leadership enables them to act with vigor in their relations with other labor unions or with other power holders in the society, thus helping to preserve the balance of power.

Collective Bargaining as Group Process and as Power Conflict

Union-management relations are often peaceful; many organized firms have never had a strike. The character of union-management contact is always, however, conditioned by the fact that union leaders and industrial management represent power organizations which can put pressure on each other to force a desired outcome. In the early stages when a union is seeking recognition there may be marked conflict. Resistance may come from the workers themselves, from a company union, or even from another union trying to organize the same plant. The strongest opposition comes from management partly because it may feel it has a great deal to lose and partly because of powerful beliefs in managerial prerogatives. Management tactics have included physical force, discharge or threat of discharge, increased liberality, anti-union propaganda and the injunction. Against such obstacles the union must use all of its strength.

The organizer has been studied by a number of persons. Karsh, Seidman and Lilienthal (1953), in a detailed report of how a small midwestern knitting mill was organized by the International Ladies' Garment Workers Union, point out the importance of the personality of the organizer. This organizer probed for dissatisfactions and then placed responsibility for them on the employer. In addition she was liked and admired by workers as a person. If such tactics fail, a strike may be called. On the other hand when the early period of organization is a peaceful one, worker attachment to the union clearly would be different. Dunlop (1960) points out that when members have been organized by a vote in a government-conducted election or by the union security provision of an agreement, they hardly will feel the same attachment to the union as the men who were organized on the picket line. After a union has been in a plant for some time and has been accepted, a special problem is presented by the need to shift from the approach of the early agitation period to one adapted to enduring negotiations. Often the agitators are still around and insist that management cannot be trusted. It then may be necessary for the union to move such agitators to parts of the country that have not yet been organized.

The inability of labor union leaders to control their membership is a source of management exasperation. Popiel (1955) points out that although a union is a bureaucracy, unlike the factory bureaucracy it must consult its members on important decisions. Often the union leader most able to behave in a businesslike manner — that is, to behave like a dependable labor contractor who can assure fulfillment of agreements — is the labor racketeer. For a consideration, such a person calls a strike against a competitor of the company or talks his own union into accepting a lower wage increase than that desired. Such racketeers are the robber barons of labor. (Mills, 1948, pp. 122-132.)

Much research, as well as scholarly discussion and reminiscences of experiences as arbitrators, has been directed at the grievance process. The contract normally will specify a special set of procedures involving a step-by-step movement up the line in case one's grievance is not taken care of at a lower level. It may provide that the issue shall be taken to arbitration, and there may be other provisions for mediation and conciliation as well. Actually, a grievance need not be initiated at the bottom. It can be initiated by anyone, however high up he might stand in the factory or the union. A worker at the bottom might not even wish to initiate a grievance, but the union grievance committee might do so if it felt an important principle was involved or if it wished to harrass management in order to obtain some other objective. The fact that top management often uses the number of grievances the foreman receives as a measure of his efficiency makes it possible for a union official to get action on a desired matter by threat such as was made to a foreman by one of Sayles and Strauss' (1953) subjects: "I've got thirteen grievances in my pocket. If you don't wise up, then you get all thirteen in the morning. Understand?" (p. 31.) On the other hand, the union itself may stop a grievance it does not regard as worth fighting for or one it may feel interferes with other matters in which it is more interested. Grievances may revolve about anything but the most common subjects are seniority, safety and health, vacation, discharge, and wages. In a sense most grievances are wage grievances of one sort or another and the wage section of the contract is probably the most important. Although there are many possibilities, there seem to be three major matters which workers clearly expect from their unions: wage improvement, (including fringe benefits), job security, and protection from arbitrary actions.

It has come to be recognized that the labor union is not simply an instrument for mediating disputes between workers and managers but has become a major institution in its own right, whose independent development affects seriously the character of the economy and the society. While the general strike has never been as significant a tactic in the United States as in Great Britain and France,

American labor unions are able to accomplish almost as much because of the fact that national unions may contain hundreds of thousands of workers and can bring key industries, such as coal mining and the automobile industry, to a virtual standstill. It is testimony to their power that the national government expresses concern about any strike as not being "in the national interest." When one or only a few national unions can bargain with far-flung industries, unions have become very powerful indeed, a fact which has led some to write of a "labor monopoly." The impact of unions on the economy and even on wages, however, is by no means obvious and is the subject of considerable controversy.

Union-management relations provide one of the most fruitful areas for the examination of social conflict. Some students have sought the explanation for that conflict in man's personality and aspirations. The basic difficulty, they say, is that man is an active creature who wants things and moves heaven and earth to try to get them. Since men want the same kinds of things, they will conflict over who gets them. Kerr and Siegel (1954), after a careful study of eleven countries, conclude that strikes (conceived as an index of conflict) were due to the workers' position in society. They write ". . .industries will be highly strike prone when the workers form a relatively homogeneous group which is unusually isolated from the general community and which is capable of cohesion; an industry will be comparatively strike free when the workers are individually integrated into the larger society, are members of trade groups which are coerced by government or the market to avoid strikes, or are so individually isolated that strike action is impossible." (Kerr and Siegel, 1954, p. 195.) Others place emphasis on economic factors such as the elasticity of product demand or the swings of the business cycle. A few attribute conflict to insecure union leadership, and some have called attention to ideological differences, seeing revolutionary unions in life-and-death battle with reactionary bosses. A few have claimed that "key" industry and pattern-bargaining create conflict. Some have pointed their fingers at certain dominant personalities like John L. Lewis and George Meany, or Lemuel Boulware and the late Senator Robert Taft.

All these explanations have merit, some more than others, but their relative explanatory power is at present a subject of controversy. The fundamental solution to conflict in union-management relations, at least in the United States, and in other countries not having centralized governments has been to avoid attacking these basic or underlying causes, turning instead to collective bargaining. There are other ways — coercion, the firing squad, brainwashing — but collective bargaining is the technique most congenial to democratic values. It is a short-run solution, but given the continuous and recurrent character of industrial conflict, a short-run approach is most practical. What is amazing about collective bargaining is how well it works so much of the time. It brings together persons of different incomes, background, race, religion and belief and makes them come to an agreement they can accept — at least for a time.

Collective bargaining recognizes that union-management relations form a power struggle. It is not assumed that disputes can be settled merely by getting together and seeing the other fellow's point of view, or by developing common attitudes and values. It does assume, however, that the bargainers are of relatively equal strength. A bargain between a big man and a small man is no bargain at all, for the strong man can force the weak man to do his will. Whyte (1961, pp. 326-328) describes a case in which management was unconvinced by the union leaders' arguments that a wage increase was required but decided to grant an increase simply out of what it made clear was the generosity of management. The result was a state of anomie in the union. Later in the year the union felt it necessary to demand a greater increase than management felt was warranted. The union and the membership regarded what management had given spontaneously as not having been won and consequently as not counting. Only by careful maneuvering was a strike avoided.

The dynamics of bargaining have been studied a great deal and the relative values of differential approaches and the poker-playing strategy called for have been the subject of considerable discussion. Should collective bargaining not result in compromise and a settlement, a strike may occur.

The strike as used by American business unions was not invented by them but was adapted to their goals. Its purpose is to lead to a settlement and continued operation of the business corporation. The contrast is seen in the goals of revolutionary unions such as those of the syndicalists and Communists. To them the union as

122

well as the strike was designed to hurt business and overthrow management completely. In contrast the American union of the present day sees the strike as one of its weapons in the bargaining process, as a way not of preventing a settlement but of speeding one up. The goal is continued work and continued capitalistic business. The evidence for this claim of the unions is of several kinds. Unions have rationalized the strike and succeeded in controlling emotional outbursts. Ross writes, "Anger and resentment are dampened when the moment is inappropriate and accentuated when the time is ripe; emotion is stored up and paid out in the light of cold strategical requirements." (Ross, 1954, p. 32.) Unions have enforced discipline so as to reduce the likelihood of strikes' getting out of hand. The eager beaver and the hothead are the natural enemies of the union official since they have a tendency to assume that every grievance must be settled here and now. The union official feels it is up to the professional to select the time and place, and therefore improvident protest movement must be avoided lest valuable contacts and relationships be sacrificed for small gains. These practices are so carefully and rationally planned that the ILGWU once put out a handbook in which methods for leaders to follow were set down in writing.

During a strike, discipline requires that every person be given a job to do — on the picket line, at union headquarters, or in the administration of strike benefits. It is particularly important that strikes be handled in a diplomatic manner and be brought to a conclusion as rapidly as possible because union members themselves are not particularly interested in long drawn-out strikes. Some recent figures put out by the AFL-CIO are interpreted by Bendiner (1961, p. 42) as follows: "A typical union member today is between 35 and 44, married ten years, and is as likely to own a home and mortgage in the suburbs as to rent a flat in the city. The chances are there is another wage earner in the family, probably part-time, raising the household income to the middle bracket. A car, a checking account, and a small savings account fill out the picture. What the survey does not say but what union leaders freely admit is that strikes are an unwelcome interruption for these credit-burdened middle-class workers. Moreover, taxes and socially oriented politics are no more popular among them than in the local Chamber of

123

Commerce. And neither union nor government gets credit from them for the various forms of social security they enjoy and take for granted. Members under 40 tend to believe that people have always had vacations with pay and that collective bargaining and social security came in with Jefferson and are part of the Constitution."

The rationalization of the strike and the discipline of the members are not the only evidence that the strike is part of the bargaining process. Strikes have been carefully adjusted to the economic and political beliefs and customs of the community. The contract is accepted as binding, and long before they were outlawed sympathetic strikes had declined from 3.7 per cent of all strikes between 1881 and 1905 to a figure of 1.1 per cent in the periods of 1937-41 and 1945-47. The strike is also conducted so as to minimize unnecessary damage to the industry, inconvenience to the community, and loss of public opinion. Other forces operate which reduce conflict and help bring the contending parties together. Government has played an increasing role, and legal devices such as conciliation, mediation, and fact-finding encourage settlement. Contributing to dispute resolution is the fact that both sides have an interest in strike settlement and an early return to work. (Dubin, 1958, b.)

There also are many cases of active union-management cooperation in the solution of particular problems to the point where unions actually take over certain activities from management, as when the ILGWU uses its own experts to work out joint time studies of production standards, design the administration of wage incentive payment plans, job evaluations, merit ratings, and the installation of work simplification techniques through motion study. The International Typographical Union legislates shop rules without management participation. In turn management provides space for meeting, may collect dues and through union shop agreements helps recruit members. None of this is to say, however, that the conflict between them is necessarily reduced or being eliminated, nor can one expect that it ever will be eliminated. As long as there are clear differences of interest on major issues, conflict will provide an index of those differences. Where differences begin to disappear one should investigate the possibility of collusion.

CHAPTER 8

MOTIVATION OF
WORK BEHAVIOR

Job Satisfaction

A careful survey of several hundred studies revealed that, on the average, only about 13 per cent of persons express dissatisfaction with their jobs. (Robinson and Connors, 1963.) Though the samples in a large proportion of these studies are wholly inadequate and the particular groups investigated are not representative in any sense, the studies are impressive by virtue of the extent to which they confirm each other. A very high portion, 80 per cent or more, of American workers apparently are satisfied with their jobs. As Blauner (1960, p. 341) puts it, such a finding is "neither particularly surprising nor sociologically interesting." One would expect persons to be positively oriented to those things that they are in fact doing, and the chances are that any over-all percentages on satisfaction with marriage, religion, nation, or state would also be, on balance, positive.

More interesting are data on occupational and industrial differences in work satisfaction. Here we find striking variations indeed. Blauner (1960) believes that four major factors account for them. Occupational prestige seems to be the one best explanatory factor, professionals being at the top, higher white-collar next, lower white-collar next, skilled manual, semiskilled and unskilled following in that order. If an occupation is evaluated highly it becomes possible for those in the occupation to continue to perform objectively unsatisfying things, such as dirty work, and yet not feel the work demeans them. Although all work involves elements of control, the relative closeness or degree of control is inversely related to job satisfaction. The amount of control is very high among the professions and very low among factory workers, whose lack of control is symbolized by the clock they must punch, an indignity avoided by even the lowliest white-collar worker. One must be careful, however, not to underestimate the satisfactions that may be present in even highly regimented work. Baldamus (1961) uses the word "traction" to refer to the rhythms and swings which highly regularized and competitive work may assume. Turner and Miclette (1962) show that workers may be caught up in these swings and be carried along with them with considerable satisfaction. On the other hand it is certainly easy to romanticize such pleasures. Degree of control would seem to be important in explaining the low job satisfaction of automobile workers compared to the higher satisfaction of miners, although the latter have lower prestige. Close supervision is related to the relatively high job satisfaction reported by truck drivers and railroad workers as compared to the lower job satisfaction of the automobile workers and others subject to close supervision.

The extent to which the task permits teamwork has been found to be related to job satisfaction. Walker (1950) attributed the principal cause of integrated work teams to the basic technological processes and the imperatives they impose. In steel making small group operations thus are required, whereas he felt on the automobile assembly line small groups were almost impossible to form.

Occupational communities (occupational association among workers off the job) also increase job satisfaction. An occupational community isolated from other parts of the society can exist in the case of mining. A similar isolation may occur when there are off-hour shifts as in the cases of the printers, steelworkers, firemen and railroad men. Where such an occupational community develops, the workers in their off hours socialize more with one another, tend to talk shop, and tend to use the occupation itself as their reference group to judge conduct.

Blauner (1960) concludes that the contrast between the picture of the happy, creative craftsmen of the past and the alienated unhappy worker of the present has been greatly exaggerated. The craftsmen of the medieval period were not typical workers, but accounted for less than 10 per cent of the medieval labor force. It was the peasant who was the representative laborer and he was, says DeMan (1929, p. 146), "practically nothing more than a working beast." By contrast much work that goes on in the modern world is far from being alienated. Thus Friedmann (Blauner, 1960, p. 360) did not find any decline in the proportion of skilled workers in German, French and English industries during the early years of the twentieth century, and statistics for the United States show that the proportion of unskilled workers and of semiskilled workers has been holding its own or declining.

The over-all picture is one of an upgrading in skill and an increase in white collar and professional workers. It is not among this latter group that alienation and job dissatisfaction are held to be particularly high. Further, as the data suggest, job dissatisfaction is far from being equally distributed even among the blue collar workers. In addition one should not assume that job satisfaction is a function primarily of the relation between the man and the job. Major elements are prestige, integrated work groups and occupational communities which are social and only indirectly related to the job itself. Roy (1959-60), describing an exceedingly dull job in which he was employed, shows how the long, boring day was made meaningful by the development of "times." The day became made up of starting time, peach time (when one of the members of the work group shared some peaches which he brought to work), lunch-time, window time, pick-up time (when a pick-up man came to remove completed parts) and so forth. The day was spent in anticipating a coming "time" and evaluating it after it was over.

Motivation

The subject of motivation has been one of the most intensely studied in the general field of work behavior. Because of our focus on industrial relations, we shall restrict our attention to the questions that arise in connection with incentive systems. This also will enable us to examine motivation theory and the research revolving about the social aspects of motivation in an industrial setting.

The usual practice is to provide an increment of reward proportional to each increment of effort, rewards extending to whatever is valued in the society (commonly money), promotion to a better position, greater responsibility and authority, opportunities to purchase company goods or stock certificates, time off, access to special facilities (such as company-owned vacation resorts), insurance, pensions, and other benefits and services. To make measurement possible, however, some monetary base is most ordinary.

The most common rewards systems are these.

A. INDIVIDUAL INCENTIVE SYSTEMS. These are of three main types. 1. piecework and standard time — the individual receives an identical and predictable amount for each unit of output; 2. shared gains — the individual receives a proportion of the value of his output beyond a standard amount (Halsey, Rowan, Bedaux systems); 3. variable return systems — the individual receives amounts per unit which differ according to his level of output (Taylor, Emerson systems). Commissions may be regarded as variants of piecework plans, though they are often highly complex. In all individual systems, the worker usually is guaranteed a minimum amount (base pay) to compensate him for times when he cannot work through no fault of his own (machinery breakdown or supply failures, for example) or the minimum may be provided because of labor union demands.

B. GROUP INCENTIVE SYSTEMS. The earnings of a group of men, such as a work crew, are pooled and each receives a proportion of the value of any output beyond a standard amount. Occasionally the group includes all or most of the employees (Rucker and Scanlon plans). Payoff occurs as a proportion of labor saved or costs reduced.

C. COLLECTIVE ARRANGEMENTS. These include profit-sharing, deferred compensation bonuses, stock purchase options, and the like. The latter shade off into fringe benefits such as pension plans, insurance, surgical plans, and other benefits or services like vaca-

tions, credit unions, athletic facilities, lunch rooms, and parking facilities. The incentive impact of most collective arrangements seems
to be tenuous owing to the relatively remote connection between
them and effect expended by the employee. Profits are pleasant to
receive but the worker can scarcely feel (and certainly not predict)
that extra effort on his part will result in a proportional profit return. An upturn in the market may return him far more. Measures
such as these are more properly conceived of as devices to secure
tax advantages (especially in the United States) and as measures to
reduce worker turnover and raise morale. Some of them may be
required by law or even provided by the government itself.

History and Distribution of Incentive Schemes

Although Karl Marx characterized piece-rates as "the form of
wages most in harmony with the capitalist mode of production,"
their use antedates modern capitalism by at least 2,000 years. Incentive systems were used by the Chaldeans as early as 400 B.C.
and probably by the Romans in the first century A.D. They are also
quite common among agricultural and peasant peoples in many
places. They began to be used widely in the West with the breakdown of the guild system and the coming of the putting-out system in the sixteenth to eighteenth centuries. The merchant provided materials for domestic work, paying for products by the piece,
a form of subcontracting that was not long in turning into employment under piecework. The spirit of such a relationship is being
drawn on by the present-day employer who speaks of his piecework employees as being "in business for themselves."

The factory system made wide use of incentive systems, primarily the individual type. Their appeal was mainly as an approach
to reducing labor costs: employers could cut rates to keep income
at a level while output increased. This fact, plus the lack of objective measures of standards of output, led to the profound hos-
tility of workers toward incentive plans (such plans being blamed
even for economic depressions) which is widespread even now,
though it is decreasing. The provision of methods for establishing
standards that were based on job analysis rather than previous
experience was one of the main contributions of Frederick W.

Taylor and his followers around the turn of the twentieth century. The assumption by this group that motivation was largely an individual matter and their arrogation of the title of "scientific management" to their measurements resulted in powerful and resentful opposition to their approach. At present it is widely recognized that job analysis and measurement, however carefully executed, involve subjective judgments, and that solutions to measurement problems often reflect little more than the relative strength of union and management or the social norms. Indeed it was recognition of the difficulty of setting minimum or average standards that helped lead to the development of the Halsey and Rowan plans. Such plans involved recognition that since a standard might be set too low, management would be discouraged from rate-cutting because it also shared in the gains.

The present use of incentive systems is difficult to measure because of lack of data. Labor unions, especially in the United States, claim they are declining but available objective studies show no decrease. From 25 per cent to 30 per cent of workers in U.S. industry (mostly in manufacturing) are estimated to be covered by incentives, a figure which appears to have remained stable since the end of World War II. This stability appears to be due to the offsetting of abandonment of incentives in some firms by the expansion of coverage in others already using them partially, rather than from wholly new adoptions. Comparison of United States with European figures is made difficult by the European practice of using "piece rate" as synonymous with the broader "incentive system"; hence, perhaps this exaggerates the European figures. Nevertheless, European figures are in general higher than those in the United States. In the United Kingdom, 42 per cent of wage earners in 1961 were on "payment by results," an increase of 8 per cent over the figure for 1938. In 1949, the proportion of hours worked in industry at piece rate was 37 per cent in West Germany, 41 per cent in Denmark, close to 60 per cent in Norway and Sweden, and 70 per cent in Hungary. The figure for Russia seems to be at least as high as that for Hungary and has been estimated to include almost all workers. Piecework is, apparently, as much "in harmony" with the communist as with the capitalist mode of production.

130

Increasing automation has led some forecasters to see the complete abandonment of incentive payments since, it is claimed, the output of self-operating, decision-making machinery is not attributable to the effort of the man who watches the dials or subjects the machinery to periodic maintenance checks. Available data, though spotty, give little support to this expectation. In fact, "equipment utilization incentives" (an incentive for keeping the machines running or for not slowing down) seem to be growing. Perhaps the best insurance that incentive systems will be utilized for a long time is the lack of effective methods for evaluating them in operation. The number of firms abandoning them for the wrong reasons will surely be offset by the number extending or adopting them for different though equally wrong reasons.

Current Theory and Research

A greater gap than is usual in science exists between research and practitioner. Students of industrial sociology, psychology, management, and industrial relations have been critical of all incentive systems, but managers of firms and personnel administrators nevertheless install them out of a belief shared in industry that they "work." Laboratory experiments, though offering the advantage of control of variables, have been inconclusive. Though old comparisons of performance by subjects "alone" and "together" (Triplett's famous experiment on the speed of winding silver cord around two fishing reels was carried out in 1898) offer inconsistent results. Usually individual productivity has been shown to be superior to group productivity for manual tasks but the structure of the group is of major significance. For example, the need for specialization, supervision, or the effects of interpersonal compatibility may be critical. On the other hand, the claimed superiority for group work arrangements over the individual often vanishes when results are calculated in number of man-minutes required to reach a solution. (Hare, 1962, Chapter 12.)

Even were the results of such experiments to point uniformly in the same direction they would bear little on industrial incentive systems, for not only are laboratory controls lacking but confounding variables make evaluation almost impossible. For the installation of an incentive system to motivate behavior it must be possible for an average worker to make a bonus over his base pay. One therefore must measure the output of an average worker. Making such measurements leads to discoveries that the job can be simplified or improved. In addition, since the workers can make a bonus only if supplies are continually forthcoming, management will take special pains to be sure there is an unbroken flow. Through such job and supply improvement, costs may indeed go down whether or not one has the incentive system. Evaluation would require separating out the effects of these changes. A promising "halfway house" between the laboratory and actual work situation is a "miniature replica model." (Wager and Palola, 1964.)

Another issue is theoretical: the relation of the incentive system to a theory of motivation. Psychologists describe motivation in terms of a set of needs or drives (inherited and acquired) which an incentive satisfies. Research therefore focuses on the discovery and description of such needs. A motive, in this view, stands back of or causes drive-reducing behavior. Sociologists see motivation as the mobilization of behavior in the pursuit of valued ends. A motive arises when behavior is interrupted and an explanation must be given. An appropriate vocabulary of motives must be acquired, the person utilizing the vocabularly appropriate to his identity. Research focuses on the social anchoring of identities. For example, rate-busters outproduce those who restrict output not because of differences in need but because of differences in identity and values. In industry there has been a strong tendency to use the psychological approach when dealing with others, the sociological when dealing with oneself. Thus when managers set up incentive systems for low-level manual workers, they use need-satisfaction schemes; when they set up systems for management, they think in terms of the identification with the firm, loyalty and other values.

Incentive Systems in Operation

Many incentive systems fail to motivate because their designers ignore the social nature of work and the active character of the person. Appeals to the isolated workers ("*You* work harder and *you* will get more") ignore his relationship to his fellows, and, in fact, operate to reduce the motivation to cooperate with work-crew members or even with management itself. An organization is not a set of disparate individuals, each competing actively with the other on independent tasks in the manner of a school class of students. An organization is instead a finely articulated flow which requires not that each person work at top speed but that each work according to plan at a required pace. Further, incentive system designers often assume the worker is a lazy organism who, in the absence of incentive, will do nothing at all or as little as possible. He must be continually jogged: hence the incentive system.

Such a pessimistic view of man represents a turning around of causation for it is itself largely responsible for producing such a man — by proceeding in the following manner. Workers, it is found, do not produce as desired by management. Instead of inquiring further, it is immediately assumed that they must be offered an inducement to do so in the form of an incentive. Workers then seek to "beat" the incentive by trying to secure a piece rate low enough to enable them to earn a larger bonus. The designers of the system respond by trying to tighten up the rates. The workers try to outwit them. After a number of such encounters, the designers conclude that workers are a lazy, undependable group who do as little as they can get away with. The supposedly lazy person undergoes a puzzling metamorphosis, however, when the 5 o'clock whistle blows; in fact, his behavior, instead of "lazy" is simply what his employers would call "economically rational" in another context.

The social nature of work makes itself felt in a variety of ways relevant to the operation of an incentive system. In the case, for example, of a group incentive system, workers are supposed to be motivated to cooperate. This they may indeed do, but they will rigidly limit this cooperation to their own work crew, excluding other work crews and management itself. For example, they will refuse to accept trainees or apprentices in their group since they will pull their average down. Management will have to undertake the training of these persons separately. Also, it is often claimed that piece rate systems reduce the need for close supervision since labor costs are self-policing: if workers slow down on the job, they will suffer for it. In reality, supervisors are likely to be judged by the bonus earned by the work group. In line with assumptions of economic rationality, it is felt that a group earning a respectable bonus is satisfied and doing a good job; if they are not earning a bonus, their morale must be low and their work inefficient. In either case, the results may be attributed to the supervisor. Supervisors thus find themselves spending far more time in supervising such a group than they would if the group were on time earnings. Supervisors may even reach the point of colluding with their men in securing loose incentive rates so their men will earn substantial bonuses.

Incentive systems often result in group conflict. Under job evaluation, it is assumed that since job A requires more education, involves more responsibility, or requires greater concentration than job B, therefore job A should be rated at $1.50 per hour while job B is rated at $1.25 per hour. Job B is on incentive, however, and it is soon discovered that the workers are earning $1.60 an hour. Management is then puzzled when a worker in job B refuses a "promotion" to job A, or maintenance men, who service the machines on which incentive workers earn bonuses, demand a share of those earnings since they feel they are partly responsible for the ouput.

Perhaps the central question lies in understanding work motivation and this forces us to relate the workers' behavior to their reference groups — the groups whose values they accept and whose norms they follow. The major clues are provided by examining restriction of output (the practice of deliberately holding down the amount, speed, or pace of production) and asking why workers are motivated to restrict. It is impossible to understand restriction unless one recognizes that it is not an individual but a group phenomon. If the individual worker were to restrict consistently he would be discharged, for his low productivity in comparison to others would be patent. Restriction is not a matter of simply holding back but of holding to an *agreed* rate: only then can a work crew avoid sanctions for restriction (though management is usually quite satisfied with their production). One would predict, and research supports the prediction, that getting workers to produce at an agreed rate takes time, cooperation, the assistance or even collusion of inspectors, time checkers, stockmen and others, and means for imposing sanctions on deviants. It is all a lot of trouble, workers end up with less money, and the whole thing is quite illegal from management's point of view and hence subjects workers to the risk of immediate discharge if discovered. Clearly, the motives that result in restriction must be very powerful.

There appear to be seven reasons for restricting according to Gross. (1958, pp. 518-528.) 1. Controlling management by securing favorable piece rates through deliberate slowdowns. If workers earn no bonus, it is hoped management will feel the rate was set too tightly and should be loosened. 2. Fear that management will cut the rates if earnings get too high. How ever rare the latter may actually be, it can happen and has indeed happened in many places. 3. Securing leisure-time at work. Once the worker has produced his "quota" he is free to relax, light his pipe, and turn to informal relations with his fellows. Such leisure-time is not "wasted": a part of it is spent in planning the next piece of work and anticipating difficulties. 4. Controlling competition so that one is not compared unfavorably with one's fellows. Such comparisons are made not only by management but by fellow workers. Through restriction, a status structure becomes stabilized and men know what to expect of one another. 5. Avoiding the sanctions suffered by the rate-buster who will be ostracized, or even physically attacked. The rate-buster is penalized in another way. Although his producing at a high rate of output implies an orientation to managerial goals, he develops a reputation for being unable to get along with others or enlist their cooperation. This reputation often disqualifies him from consideration for promotion to a supervisory position. 6. Giving meaning to work (through the fact of partially controlling competition and through making a "poor" job yield a bonus). 7. The seventh reason is one of which workers and managers are largely unconscious. Research suggests a difference in the structure of the aspirations of middle class persons on the one hand and working-class persons on the other. The former are oriented to success and achievement, and to deferred gratification; the latter are oriented to holding on to their jobs, raising their children so that they can hold jobs and do not get into "trouble," and to the enjoyment of the company of their families and immediate friends. It seems clear that individual incentive plans will be much more appealing to the former than to the latter. In any case, the real chance that a working-class person can raise his wage (base pay) appreciably by own effort is not large (the range for his job is usually narrow and he reaches the top very early in his career), and his chance of promotion (as a reward) is even smaller. After a few years of trying, he therefore is likely to turn to other values, perhaps leaving to a union or a political party the task of keeping his earnings proportional to the cost of living.

These seven factors obviously are potent and will hardly disappear because an incentive scheme offers the chance to earn an extra 10 per cent per hour. On the other hand, where incentive systems work best, they have been tied to the workers' values. Examples include their relatively successful use in the commission system for salesmen, in bonuses for management, in the favorable responses of rate-busters (who, though a small group, do have values which are more like those of management than of their fellows), and in situations where effort bears a relation to strongly-sensed societal goals. Productivity goes up in wartime, or when workers feel a relationship between what they do and national values they hold dear (as in incentive systems in some totalitarian countries or utopian communities), or if their work is a sign of grace or means to heaven.

The individual reward system that seems to come closest to tying incentives to worker values is the Scanlon plan. (Lesieur, 1958.) Its main feature is a structure which provides for labor-management cooperation and consultation, is labor-saving and provides for adoption of worker suggestions. Restriction of output seems to be low under this plan.

The relative success of incentive systems is also related to the market or community in which the industry must operate. If the incentive system results in increased production, then demand for the product must be elastic or inventories will pile up. Indeed, the fear that this may happen (and workers be laid off) motivates workers to keep production down. In some industries — the needle trades of New York City provide the best example — the piece work system is universal because of the very stiff competition among the many small firms, because of tradition, and because of its acceptance by the unions who are largely responsible for the stability of the industry.

Incentive systems have many latent effects. They put pressure on management to evaluate jobs more carefully, to supervise with greater rationality, to provide more dependable supplies, to inspect products more closely, to seek out specialists in job evaluation, wage and salary administration, time and motion study, accounting, and other functions. How ever well or poorly the incentive system works, management may thus be doing a more efficient job. At the same time, the personnel department becomes a more significant element in the organization. Incentive systems are often also an attractive feature in recruiting new workers. Whether these considerations justify incentive systems is a moot question.

Much of the objection to industrial reward systems is rational and based on the kinds of problems to which we have alluded. The amount of emotional opposition has greatly declined. Labor unions are more sympathetic than they have been, and even join in the task of evaluating jobs and setting rates, an activity they can hardly avoid if they wish to serve their members. In addition, the emphasis in the 1960's on international competition has led to great pressure to stimulate productivity in the national interest. Underdeveloped countries aspire to a standard of living equal to that of the richest countries and are searching for ways of unleashing the productive potential of their peoples. Leaders often introduce Western incentive systems only to encounter powerful opposition from native values, for the individualism of these schemes often runs counter to loyalties to family, religion, tribe or casts. The dilemma may be whether the leaders can alter those values when their leadership rests on the fact that they embody them. In many countries, however, the traditional values are changing anyhow, or else governments, possessed of a monopoly of the means of violence, ruthlessly destroy them. Westerners sometimes question the efficiency of incentive systems which rest on the whip and the firing squad. They will work, some say, in only the short run, but perhaps they are overestimating the time needed to develop an industrial system, and the foundation of a high standard of living. The new countries are in a hurry.

The data do not permit us to conclude that the use of industrial reward systems, on a world-wide scale, is increasing or decreasing, or whether they will necessarily increase productivity or lower costs. Pieceworkers usually outproduce those paid on a straight-time basis (other variables are rarely controlled) but such gains are at least partly offset by the costs of installation and administration of the system (time study, extra inspections for quality, job evaluation, etc.). Clearly more research is needed both under laboratory conditions and in realistic field situations. The questions of policy and societal values to which we have referred suggest that the subject will still require public discussion, intuitive judgment and imaginative solutions.

Man and Organization: The Costs of Efficiency

Within recent years a growing number of critics of modern organization have called attention to what they feel are the great costs of organization in the form of pressures on the individual and restrictions on his creativity (Argyris, 1957; Herzberg, 1960; Maier, 1955; Maslow, 1954; McGregor, 1960; Whyte, 1956.) The claim that organizations have harmful effects on the individual has been called by Strauss (1963) the "personality versus organization theory."

The basic principles of this theory can be stated as follows:

It is assumed that humans have certain needs they carry into all situations that confront them. There are many schemes of needs but the most popular is that put forth by Maslow (1943). The latter claims that there are five needs arranged in a hierarchy as follows:

5. self-actualization
4. esteem
3. social satisfaction
2. safety
1. physical well-being

It is maintained that a higher need does not motivate unless all of the lower needs below it are satisfied. Further, once a need is satisfied it no longer motivates the individual. Physical needs must be satisfied first. Once these are satisfied, usually through gainful employment in our society, the person will become more concerned with his other needs. He will be concerned with safety by seeking security through seniority and other fringe benefits. Once those needs are realized he can turn to his needs for friendship and group support. It is assumed then that hungry men have little interest in whether or not their working companions are satisfactory. One must be relatively well-off before one even begins to worry about such things. When all of the lower needs are satisfied the person can turn to the highest one of all: self-actualization. This need is not described with clarity but it is the one which occupies the greatest attention of these thinkers. Maslow himself describes self-actualization as "the desire to become more and more what one is, to become everything one is capable of becoming . . . a musician must make music, an artist must paint, a poet must write, if he is to be ultimately happy. What a man *can* be he *must* be." Maslow (1943, p. 372).

It is maintained that healthy persons desire to mature. Maturing means moving up the hierarchy of needs; that is, not being satisfied to take care only of the needs for physical well-being or safety. Being completely mature means taking care of the need to actualize one's self through creativeness, autonomy, the use of discretion, independence, and thus to express one's unique personality with freedom.

The attempt on the part of the person to express his unique personality runs into severe opposition from organizations, particularly large-scale ones. By definition, organizations seek to reduce discretion and creativity, to control and direct behavior. In contrast to the person's needs, organizations demand conformity, obedience and dependence and hence keep the person at an immature level. The favorite citations are studies of assembly line workers, engineers, and the business executive and manager. The latter has, perhaps, been most celebrated because of the popularity of the work by Whyte (1956) which gave birth to the phrase the "organization man." Whyte maintains that the emphasis on conformity and obedience is found not only in organizations but infects the entire society, child-rearing techniques, literature, residential practices, government and political ideologies as well. He cites, as an outstanding example, the point of view put forth in the novel *The*

Caine Mutiny. In this book the moral question is put as follows: What does one do if one is on board a boat in time of war when one's captain is a martinet, when he is a coward, a thief, a schizophrenic and clearly incompetent? What does one do when this person is in command of the boat during a storm at sea and when, through his command, the boat is in danger of foundering and one is in danger of losing one's life? The answer given is that one must continue to obey the man in spite of one's reservations, for to question authority — to question rules or orders in organizations even though they go against one's own wishes or one's own needs — is to call into doubt the structure itself and consequently to reduce its ability to accomplish its goals. The organization therefore says: obey the rule or order no matter what your personal needs may be.

Since these needs continue to press for satisfaction the attempt to frustrate them will produce various pathological reactions. Some persons will fight back and will exhibit sabotage, output restriction, union activity and other forms of rational as well as aggressive behavior. Others will withdraw, regress, engage in childish behavior, or try to do as little work as they can. Management therefore finds that even to bring workers up to minimum standards it must impose still more restrictions just to keep the workers in line. It will install a rule which says "Obey all rules" and attempt to secure obedience to that rule. This produces even more disobedience and so on, in a vicious cycle. For some the pressure may become so great that they break down and exhibit various forms of mental disturbance or psychosomatic disorders. The result is a great battle between the organization and the individual to get the latter to alter his personality; of course since the needs are unalterable the person must fight back or collapse.

Those who present the picture that we have just given suggest various alternatives. In the main, since they lay the blame for this presumed state of affairs at the door of the organization, they insist that it is the organization that must do the changing on the assumption that individual needs are invariable. An example of the approach suggested is that offered by Herzberg and his colleagues (1960). They distinguish between what they call *hygienic factors* and *motivating factors*. Hygienic factors refer to harmonious interpersonal relations, good working conditions, good wage and salary, enlightened company policies and administrative practices, various benefits and job security. Motivating factors consist of challenging work, autonomy and interesting work (these come close to self-actualization in work). Herzberg maintains that if the hygienic factors are provided, all that will happen will be that the employees will not be unhappy; however, they will not be motivated to produce at a high level. If deprived of these factors they will complain and feel dissatisfied. On the other hand if these are provided they will simply feel that this is no more than their due. These hygienic factors take care of only the lower needs and do not touch the need for self-actualization. Instead, Herzberg maintains one must provide the motivating factors if one wishes high production.

The way in which one can solve the organization individuals' dilemma is therefore to promote intrinsic job satisfaction, individual development and work creativity. They thus will willingly work toward organization objectives because they enjoy their work and it enables them to develop. Specifically this calls for job enlargement, general supervision, decentralization, and participation by employees in decision-making.

This position is becoming increasingly popular. It is essential therefore to attempt to balance the picture by pointing out that in their attempts to criticize the impact of organizations on the individual, these theorists present as unbalanced a picture as do the enthusiasts for organization who pay no attention to its unhappy effects. Strauss (1963) presents a critique of the position which helps to balance the picture.

First, Strauss points out, the personality versus organization theorists are guilty of overemphasis on the uniqueness of the problem in large organizations. There is an inevitable conflict between the individual and the group, the individual and environment, between desire and reality. This is not to be laid at the door of large-scale organization but rather is the consequence of the discipline that is required by *any* form of organized activity. Insofar as one desires the goals of such organized activity, one must agree to submit to whatever discipline is necessary to obtain those goals.

The best place to observe the tyranny of organization over the individual is *not* in the large organization but in the small group as exemplified by the family, the small town, a group of friends,

141

a fraternity, the clique. These are the groups that do not tolerate any variation, any deviation from the values or from the party line. In a very real sense, then, organizations offer a major protection from this tyranny through the very rules to which the personality-versus-organization theorists object. Rules, after all, are the considered solutions for recurring problems. Rules do restrict the individual but they also protect him from arbitrary action and the invasion of privacy. Knowing what the rules are he must obey them, but once having obeyed them he knows that his obligations to the group are fulfilled. On the other hand, in situations where rules do not exist the person is placed in the position of dependence on other persons. He never knows when he has satisfied them and consequently can enjoy no sense of relief at knowing he has done his job. His job will be done when others say it is done and not any sooner. Such a tyranny is equivalent to slavery.

A second criticism of the personality-versus-organization position is its tendency to exaggerate the limitations of large organizations on personal freedom and on the sense of autonomy. There is a considerable literature on alienation dealing with the sense of powerlessness of the worker in the face of large-scale standardized industry and organization. Often a comparison is made between the old time craftsmen who did the whole job and the mass production worker today. This is an unfair comparison. Actually only a very small proportion of the workers in the middle ages were craftsmen, so that what one is doing is comparing the best conditions of the middle ages to the worst conditions of modern times. During the middle ages the typical worker was a peasant who, as we have noted above, was little better than a "working beast." It is certainly doubtful that the medieval serf or the Egyptian slave enjoyed much of a sense of autonomy or creativity.

We do not have data on historical shifts in job satisfaction but there have been a large number of studies in recent years. As we pointed out above, the average per cent expressing dissatisfaction with their jobs was only 13 per cent. Further this median has fluctuated between 12 and 13 per cent for over a decade. Of course these studies differ in degree of sophistication and controls, but when one has such a large number of studies they began to assume considerable validity. One can of course quarrel with the general conclusion of such study, which is that most workers are satisfied with their jobs. It is difficult to get reliable data on job satisfaction. In addition, in our society there is a strong tendency for persons to express satisfaction with their jobs. Because of the importance of work to the individual, to express dissatisfaction with one's job simply raises the question of why one does not change one's job. In spite, however, of the questions that could be raised, if the worker is supposed to be such a miserable, alienated, unhappy wretch, then the evidence certainly does not support it. The evidence is overwhelmingly the other way. The supporters of alienation theory therefore will have to offer evidence. The burden of proof is on them.

A third criticism has to do with how universal, in fact, is the need for self-actualization. It is difficult to separate the objective elements from the biases and value judgments of those holding the position. They make use of terms such as "individual dignity," "creative freedom," "self development" and the like which often are items in a set of beliefs rather than objective findings. Strauss suggests that the emphasis on such values betrays the academic origin of this theory, for such matters as creativity are particularly dear to academicians. The bulk of the population probably do not share these values and probably would not be happy at all in academic positions. From this point of view the theory starts where it ought to finish. The claim is made that self-actualization is universal. Actually it should be offered as a *conclusion* from many empirical studies rather than as a flat assertion. The claim could certainly be made that for most persons security and predictability, especially in their work, is more important than self-actualization. That does not mean they do not desire self-actualization but that they may secure it in their families, their recreation or in other areas, and not necessarily in their work.

Even if self-actualization were essential there would be little one could do to provide it for a high proportion of the population. If persons possess feelings of dependence these surely have been internalized and become part of their reaction patterns. Intensive psychotherapy would be required to produce any change. To throw such a person into challenging situations would be terrifying to him and might very well increase his dependence. Furthermore the findings of the impact of organization on mental health do not give much comfort to the personality-versus-organization theorist. Actually disturbances of mental health and psychosomatic disorders are found throughout industry and in all positions; they are found in some of their most intense forms among scientists and other professionals, and among managers who have more opportunity than most to realize their creative needs. A major study by Hinkle (1963) and his associates of the lifetime health patterns of 3,000 persons suggests that those persons who are changing jobs, who are moving up the ladder and who are presented with the most challenging opportunities are *most* likely to suffer from various mental disorders and other disturbances, rather than those who are dependent and conformist.

A fourth criticism is the tendency of the theory to overemphasize the importance of work to the individual. Clearly if the organization has such a great impact on needs it would have to be an important part of the individual's life. A person would permit these horrors to be perpetrated on him only if his work were very important to him. This does happen in some professions or occupations where the sense of vocation or mission is very strong. In most organizations, however, nothing like any great change of one's personality is really demanded and the job is not nearly so important to the individual. The central focus of a man's life may be not his job but his home or community (Dubin, 1956; Orzack, 1959).

The theory tends to underemphasize economic rewards. In the attempt to offset the traditional overemphasis on money as the major motivator, the theory goes to the other extreme. In Herzberg's work, money is listed as one of the hygienic factors rather than as one of the motivators, yet certainly money is a means for the satisfaction of all of the needs whatever they are. Furthermore it is not unimportant even in the professions. It is necessary to pay professionals a great deal of money in order to be sure that their work will not be influenced by money. There is little evidence that money ever ceases to be a motivator no matter what one's needs may be.

Finally, the supporters of this position argue on the relative costliness of the organization's impact on the individual. They argue that failing to satisfy needs is costly to both the individual and the organization. Presumably then self-actualization or autonomy, if provided, would cost less. The cost claim is most interesting. The values of the personality-versus-organization analysts revolve around autonomy, freedom, self-actualization, challenge, and achievement. These all have a strongly democratic ring. To make it even more obvious, they devalue autocratic, authoritarian structures. If these theorists therefore simply said that one *should* provide workers with more challenge or autonomy because that is consistent with democratic values, then one could not argue with them. They do not say that, however, nor can they. If they were to rest their case on such an assertion then this would not be a scientific theory but a program for the organization. Instead they say that one should provide more challenge and autonomy because it is *more efficient* to do so. One can examine the truth of that claim.

They claim that traditional organization methods lead to dissatisfaction, anxiety and aggression or to dependency, conformity, and doing only a minimum of work. The implication is that these are costly or harmful to the individual and the organization. How costly are they in fact? There is no question that, if carried to excess, anxiety, dissatisfaction, and aggression are costly, but a certain amount of them are not only unavoidable but necessary and helpful. Anxiety is the means whereby the individual is mobilized for action. Aggression is normal and healthy when the individual is confronted with threat. Dissatisfaction is where one begins in making change, including those that are absolutely essential.

It is harder to make a positive case for dependency and conformity but even there it is easy to exaggerate the possible cost gains from independence and creativity. On many jobs creative and original persons are a positive liability. The outstanding illustration would be assembly line work. Here one does not want the worker to demonstrate initiative. One does not want him to work faster, nor does one want him to work slower. One wants him simply to work according to an established pace. Creativity, then, is not always desirable. In fact most organizations, by their very nature, involve a set of prescriptions on role behavior and these involve expectations as to what each person is supposed to do. He may exercise some initiative but only within certain limits. So it is in the conduct of an orchestra. If each person attempted to exercise his own initiative in the playing of a symphony, wholesale chaos would result. In addition persons would not necessarily feel better for having satisfied personal needs.

If one looks more closely at organizations one discovers that there is creativity, originality and self-development being exhibited continually. For example the worker who restricts output, who attempts to hide original contributions which he might make to management, who works very hard to save a half hour which he can then spend loafing, is in fact demonstrating great originality. Similarly those who spend their time in industry battling for a better power position and playing politics are also demonstrating remarkable originality and expressing their creativity although it may be expressed in such a form as reducing someone else's chance for promotion or getting an undesirable person pushed out of the way or even fired. When this is pointed out many supporters of the personality-versus-organization theory claim that that is not the *kind* of originality of which they are speaking. To insist that one is only talking of *desirable* originality is to beg the whole question, however, for then one will have conceded that the organization does *not* squash the individual. The problem then becomes: how does one get persons to behave in the way in which one wishes, and that is essentially a problem in social control and not one in creativity or in the frustration of personal needs.

In sum, the personality-versus-organization theory errs insofar as it overstates its case. It is indeed true that organizations have an impact on the persons in them and that they do not attain their remarkable goals free of any cost. Some of these costs are undesirable and should certainly be eliminated or reduced as far as possible. They will not be eliminated completely, however, unless one is willing to give up the organizations themselves and the goals that they enable us to attain.

REFERENCES

ABEGGLEN, J. C. *The Japanese Factory*. Glencoe, Ill.: The Free Press, 1958.

ADAMS, G. *Workers on Relief*. New Haven: Yale University Press, 1939.

ADAMS, S. N. Status congruency as a variable in small group performance. *Social Forces*, 32, 1953-54, 16-22.

ALDOUS, JOAN. Urbanization, the extended family, and kinship ties in West Africa. *Social Forces*, 41, 1962, 6-12.

ANDERSON, N. *Work and Leisure*. New York: The Free Press of Glencoe, 1961.

ANDERSON, T. R., AND WARKOV, S. Organizational size and functional complexity. *American Sociological Review*, 26, 1961, 23-28.

ARCHIBALD, K. *Wartime Shipyard*. Berkeley and Los Angeles: University of California Press, 1947.

ARENDT, HANNAH. *The Human Condition*. Chicago: University of Chicago Press, 1958.

ARENSBERG, C. M. Industry and the community. *American Journal of Sociology*, 48, 1942, 1-12.

ARENSBERG, C. M., AND KIMBALL, S. T. *Family and Community in Ireland*. Cambridge: Harvard University Press, 1948.

ARGYRIS, C. *Organization of a Bank*. New Haven, Conn.: Labor and Management Center, Yale University, 1954. (a).

ARGYRIS, C. Human relations in the bookkeeping department. *Banking*, 46, January, 1954, 52-53 and 108-112. (b).

ARGYRIS, C. *Diagnosing Human Relations in Organizations: A Case Study of a Hospital*. New Haven, Conn.: Labor Management Center, Yale University, 1956.

ARGYRIS, C. *Personality and Organization*. New York: Harper, 1957.

ARGYRIS, C. Understanding human behavior in organizations: one viewpoint. In Haire, M. (ed.) *Modern Organization Theory*. New York: Wiley, 1959, Chapter 5.

ARGYRIS, C. *Interpersonal Competence and Organizational Effectiveness*. Homewood, Ill.: The Dorsey Press and Richard D. Irwin, 1962.

AXELROD, M. Urban structure and social participation. *American Sociological Review*, 21, 1956, 13-18.

BAKKE, E. W. *Citizens Without Work*. New Haven: Yale University Press, 1939.

BAKKE, E. W. *Principles of Adaptive Human Behavior*. New Haven: Labor and Management Center, Yale University, July, 1946.

BAKKE, E. W. *Bonds of Organization*. New York: Harper, 1950.

BAKKE, E. W. *Adaptive Human Behavior*. New Haven, Conn.: Labor and Management Center, Yale University, 1951.

BAKKE, E. W. *The Fusion Process*. New Haven, Conn.: Labor and Management Center, Yale University, 1953.

BAKKE, E. W. Concept of the social organization. In Haire, M. (ed.) *Modern Organizational Theory*. New York: Wiley, 1959, Chapter 2.

BALDAMUS, W. *Efficiency and Effort*. London: Tavistock, 1961.

BARNARD, C. I. *The Functions of the Executive*. Cambridge: Harvard University Press, 1938.

BARRETT, E. B. *The Jesuit Enigma*. New York: Boni and Liveright, 1927.

BEANE, K. D., AND SHEATS, P. Functional roles of group members. *Journal of Social Issues*, 4, 1948, 41-50.

BECKER, H., GEER, BLANCHE, HUGHES, E. C., AND STRAUSS, A. L. *Boys in White*. Chicago: University of Chicago Press, 1961.

BELL, D. *The End of Ideology*. New York: The Free Press of Glencoe, 1960. (a).

BELL, D. Discussion of Bernstein's "Union Growth and Structural Cycles." In Galenson, W., and Lipset, S. M. (eds.) *Labor and Trade Unionism*. New York: Wiley, 1960. pp. 89-93. (b).

BELSHAW, C. C. Adaptation of personnel policies in social context. In Moore, W. E., and Feldman, A. S. (eds.) *Labor Commitment and Social Change in Developing Areas*. New York: Social Science Research Council, 1960. Chapter 6.

BENDINER, R. What's wrong in the house of labor? *The Reporter*. Oct. 12, 1961, pp. 41-46.

BENDIX, R. Bureaucratization in industry. In Kornhauser, A., Dubin, R., and Ross, A. M. (eds.) *Industrial Conflict*. New York: McGraw-Hill, 1954, Chapter 12.

BENDIX, R. *Work and Authority in Industry*. New York: Wiley, 1956.

BENDIX, R. Industrialization, ideologies, and social structure. *American Sociological Review*, 24, 1959, 613-623.

BENNIS, W. G., BERKOWITZ, N., AFFINITO, M., AND MALONE, M. Reference groups and loyalties in the out-patient department. *Administrative Science Quarterly*, 2, 1958, 481-500.

BERGER, B. M. *Working Class Suburb*. Berkeley and Los Angeles: University of California Press, 1960.

BERGER, B. The sociology of leisure: some suggestions. *Industrial Relations*. 1, 1962, 31-45. (a).

BERGER, B. M. On Talcott Parsons. *Commentary*. 6, 1962, 507-513. (b).

BERLE, A. A., AND MEANS, G. C. *The Modern Corporation and Private Property*. New York: Macmillan, 1933.

148

BERLINER, J. S. *Factory and Manager in the USSR*. Cambridge, Mass.: Harvard University Press, 1957.

BERNSTEIN, I. The growth of American unions. *American Economic Review*, 44, 1954, 301-318. (a).

BERNSTEIN, I. Union growth and structural cycles. *Industrial Relations Research Association*, 1954, 202-230. (b).

BLAU, P. W. *The Dynamics of Bureaucracy*. Chicago: University of Chicago Press, 1955.

BLAU, P. W., AND SCOTT, W. R. *Formal Organizations*. San Francisco: Chandler, 1962.

BLAUNER, R. Work satisfaction and industrial trends in modern society. In Galenson, W., and Lipset, S. M. (eds). *Labor and Trade Unionism*. New York: Wiley, 1960. pp. 339-360.

BLAUNER, R. *Alienation and Freedom: The Manual Worker in Industry*. Unpublished manuscript. Berkeley, California, July, 1962.

BOULDING, K. E. *Conflict and Defense*. New York: Harper, 1962.

BUCKINGHAM, W. S., JR. Testimony in *Automation and Technological Change*. Washington: U.S. Government Printing Office, 1955. pp. 29-37.

BUNZEL, J. H. *The American Small Businessman*. New York: Knopf, 1962.

BURKE, K. *Permanence and Change*. New York: New Republic, 1935.

BURNHAM, J. *The Managerial Revolution*. New York: John Day, 1941.

CANTRIL, H., AND STRUNK, MILDRED (eds.). *Public Opinion 1935-1946*. Princeton: Princeton University Press, 1951.

CAPLOW, T. *The Sociology of Work*. Minneapolis: University of Minnesota Press, 1954.

CAPLOW, T. Organizational size. *Administrative Science Quarterly*, 1, 1957, 484-505.

CAPLOW, T. L'adaptation à la retraité chez les travailleurs de l'industrie: résultats et interprétation d'une enquête américaine. Communication to the Industry Sociology Group (Centre d'Études sociologiques), 4 March 1955. Cited in Friedmann, G. *The Anatomy of Work*. New York: The Free Press of Glencoe, 1961, p. 130.

CAPLOW, T., AND McGEE, R. J. *The Academic Marketplace*. New York: Basic Books, 1958.

CATTON, W. R., Jr. "Unstated Goals as a Source of Stress in an Organization," *Pacific Sociological Review*, 5, 1962, 29-35.

CHAPPLE, E. D., AND SAYLES, L. R. *The Measure of Management*. New York: Macmillan, 1961.

CHINOY, E. *Automobile Workers and the American Dream*. Garden City, N. Y.: Doubleday, 1955.

CLARK, B. R. *Adult Education in Transition*. Berkeley: University of California Press, 1958.

CLARK, B. R. *The Open Door College*. New York: McGraw-Hill, 1960.

CLARK, J. V. *A Preliminary Investigation of Some Unconscious Assumptions Affecting Labor Efficiency in Eight Supermarkets*. D.B.A. thesis, Harvard Graduate School of Business Administration, 1958. Cited in Homans, G. C., *Social Behavior: Its Elementary Forms*. New York: Harcourt Brace, 1961, pp. 255-262.

References

COLEMAN, J. R. The compulsive pressures of democracy in unionism. *American Journal of Sociology*, 61, 1956, 519-526.

COMMONS, J. R. American shoemakers, 1648-1895, a sketch of industrial evolution. *Quarterly Journal of Economics*, 24, 1910, 39-84.

COMMONS, J. R. *Legal Foundations of Capitalism*. Madison, Wis.: University of Wisconsin Press, 1959. First published in 1924.

COREY, L. Problems of the Peace: IV The middle class. *Antioch Review*, 5, 1945, 68-87.

COSER, L. *The Functions of Social Conflict*. Glencoe, Ill.: The Free Press, 1956.

COSER, ROSE LAUB. Authority and decision-making in a hospital. *American Sociological Review*, 23, 1958, 56-63.

CUBER, J. F., AND KENKEL, W. F. *Social Stratification in the United States*. New York: Appleton-Century-Crofts, 1954.

CYERT, R. M., AND MARCH, J. G. *A Behavioral Theory of the Firm*. Englewood Cliffs, N. J.: Prentice-Hall, 1963.

DALTON, M. Conflicts between staff and line managerial officers. *American Sociological Review*, 15, 1950, 342-351.

DALTON, M. *Men Who Manage*. New York: Wiley, 1959.

DAVIS, A. The motivation of the under-privileged worker. In Whyte, W. F. (ed.) *Industry and Society*. New York: McGraw-Hill, 1946.

DAVIS, A. K. Bureaucratic patterns in the Navy officer corps. *Social Forces*. 27, 1948, 143-153.

DAVIS, K. *Human Relations at Work*. New York: McGraw-Hill, 1962.

DAVIS, K., AND GOLDEN, HILDA H. Urbanization and the development of pre-industrial areas. In Hatt, P. K., and Reiss, A. J., Jr. (eds.) *Cities and Society*. (Revised edition) Glencoe, Ill.: The Free Press, 1957, pp. 120-140.

DE GRAZIA, S. *Of Time, Work and Leisure*. New York: Twentieth Century Fund, 1962.

DEMAN, H. *Joy in Work*. London: Allen and Unwin, 1929.

DIEBOLD, J. *Testimony in Automation and Technological Change*. Washington: U. S. Government Printing Office, 1955. pp. 6-29.

DOBRINER, W. H. (ed.) *The Suburban Community*. New York: Putnam, 1958.

DOBRINER, W. M. *Class in Suburbia*. Englewood Cliffs, N. J.: Prentice-Hall, 1963.

The Dock Worker. Liverpool, England: University Press of Liverpool, 1954.

DRUCKER, P. F. *America's Next Twenty Years*. New York: Harper, 1957.

DUBIN, R. Industrial workers' worlds: a study of the "Central Life Interests" of industrial workers. *Social Problems*, 3, 1956, 131-142.

DUBIN, R. Working Union-Management Relations. Englewood Cliffs, N. J.: Prentice-Hall, 1958.

DUNCAN, O. D., AND HODGE, R. W. Education and occupational mobility: a regression analysis. *American Journal of Sociology*, 68, 1963, 629-644.

DUNLOP, J. T. *Industrial Relations Systems*. New York: Holt-Dryden, 1958.

DUNLOP, J. T. Structural changes in the American labor movement and industrial relations system. In Galenson, W., and Lipset, S. M. *Labor and Trade Unionism*. New York: Wiley, 1960, pp. 102-116.

DURKHEIM, E. Some notes on occupational groups. In *The Division of Labor in Society.* Translated by George Simpson. Glencoe, Ill.: The Free Press, 1947. Preface to second edition.

EISENBERG, P., AND LAZARSFELD, P. F. The psychological effects of unemployment. *Psychological Bulletin,* 35, 1938, 358-390.

ELKIN, F. The soldier's language. *American Journal of Sociology,* 51, 1946, 414-422.

ELLSWORTH, J. S. *Factory Folkways.* New Haven: Yale University Press, 1952.

EMERSON, R. M. "Power-Dependence Relations," *American Sociological Review,* 27, 1962, 31-41.

ETZIONI, A. Industrial sociology: the study of economic organizations. *Social Research,* 25, 1958, 303-324.

ETZIONI, A. Authority structure and organizational effectiveness. *Administrative Science Quarterly,* 4, 1959, 43-67.

ETZIONI, A. *A Comparative Analysis of Complex Organizations.* New York: The Free Press of Glencoe, 1961.

ETZIONI, A., *Modern Organizations,* Englewood Cliffs, N. J., Prentice-Hall, 1964.

FARIS, R. E. L. Interaction of generations and family stability. *American Sociological Review,* 12, 1947, 159-164.

FAUNCE, W. A. Automation in the automobile industry: some consequences for in-plant social structure. *American Sociological Review,* 23, 1958, 401-407.

FELD, M. D. Information and authority: the structure of military organization. *American Sociological Review,* 24, 1959, 15-22.

FELLIN, P., AND LITWAK, E. Neighborhood cohesion under conditions of mobility. *American Sociological Review,* 28, 1963, 364-376.

FICHLANDER, T. C. The labor force. In Dewhurst, J. F. and Associates (eds.) *America's Needs and Resources.* New York: Twentieth Century Fund, 1955, pp. 721-734.

FLEISHMANN, E. A., HARRIS, E. F., AND BURTT, H. E. *Leadership and Supervision in Industry*: An evaluation of a Supervisory Training Program. Columbus, Ohio: Bureau of Educational Research, The Ohio State University, Monograph No. 33, 1955.

FOOTE, N. N. The Professionalization of labor in Detroit. *American Journal of Sociology,* 58, 1953, 371-380.

FORM, W. H., AND DANSEREAU, H. K. Union member orientations and patterns of social integration. *Industrial and Labor Relations Review,* 11, 1957, 3-12.

FORM, W. H., AND MILLER, D. C. Occupational career pattern as a sociological instrument. *American Journal of Sociology,* 54, 1949, 317-329.

FORM, W. H., AND MILLER, D. C. *Industry, Labor and Community.* New York: Harper, 1960.

FREUD, S. *Civilization and Its Discontents.* Hogarth Press, 1930.

FRIEDRICH, C. J. Some observations on Weber's analysis of bureaucracy. In Merton, R. K. *et al. Reader in Bureaucracy.* Glencoe, Ill.: The Free Press, 1952, pp. 27-33.

FRIEDMANN, G. *The Anatomy of Work.* New York: The Free Press of Glencoe, 1961.

151

References

FROMM, E. *Marx's Concept of Man*. New York: Frederick Ungar, 1961.

GAY, E. F. Putting-out system. In *Encyclopedia of the Social Sciences*, 13, 1932, 7-11.

GERTH, H., AND MILLS, C. W. A Marx for the managers. *Ethics*. 52, 1942, 200-215.

GERTH, H., AND MILLS, C. W. (translation) From Max Weber: *Essays in Sociology*. New York: Oxford University Press, 1946.

GIBBS, J. P., AND MARTIN, W. T. Urbanization, technology, and the division of labor: international patterns. *American Sociological Review*, 27, 1962, 667-677.

GLOVER, J. D. *The Attack on Big Business*. Cambridge, Mass.: Harvard University Press, 1954.

GOFFMAN, E. *The Presentation of Self in Everyday Life*. Garden City, N. Y.: Doubleday, 1959.

GOLDNER, F. H. Organizations and their environment: roles at their boundary. Unpublished paper read at meetings of American Sociological Society, New York, 1960. Cited in Blau, P., and Scott, W. R. *Formal Organizations*. San Francisco: Chandler, 1962, p. 197.

GOULDNER, A. W. Red tape as a social problem. In Merton, R. K. *et al. Reader in Bureaucracy*. Glencoe, Ill.: The Free Press, 1952, pp. 410-418.

GOULDNER, A. W. *Patterns of Industrial Bureaucracy*. Glencoe, Ill.: The Free Press, 1954. (a).

GOULDNER, A. W. *Wildcat Strike*. Yellow Springs, Ohio: Antioch Press, 1954. (b).

GOULDNER, A. W. Cosmopolitans and locals: toward an analysis of latent social roles — I and II. *Administrative Science Quarterly*, 2, 1957-58, 281-306 and 444-480.

GOULDNER, A. W. The norm of reciprocity: a preliminary statement. *American Sociological Review*, 25, 1960, 161-178.

GOULDNER, A. W. Comment on "Managerial succession in complex organizations," *American Journal of Sociology*, 68, 1962, 54-56.

GREENFIELD, S. M. Industrialization and the family in sociological theory. *American Journal of Sociology*, 67, 1961, 321-322.

GROSS, C. *The Gild Merchant*. Oxford: Clarendon, 1890.

GROSS, E. Some functional consequences of primary controls in formal work organizations. *American Sociological Review*, 18, 1953, 368-373.

GROSS, E. *Work and Society*. New York: Crowell, 1958.

GROSS, E. The occupational variable as a research category. *American Sociological Review*, 24, 1959, 640-649.

GROSS, E. Dimensions of leadership. *Personnel Journal*, 40, 1961, 213-228

GROSS, E. Sources of lateral authority in personnel departments. *Industrial Relations*, 3, 1964, 121-133.

GUEST, R. H. Managerial succession in complex organizations. *American Journal of Sociology*, 68, 1962, 47-54. (a).

GUEST, R. H. *Organizational Change: The Effect of Successful Leadership*. Homewood, Ill.: Irwin-Dorsey, 1962. (b).

GURSSLIN, O. R., AND ROACH, J. L. Some issues in training the unemployed. *Social Problems*, 12, 1964, 86-98.

GRUSKY, O. Corporate size, bureaucratization, and managerial succession. *American Journal of Sociology*, 67, 1961, 261-269.

HALL, O. Types of medical careers. *American Journal of Sociology*, 53, 1948, 327-336.

HARBISON, F., AND MYERS, C. A. *Management in the Industrial World, An International Analysis*. New York: McGraw-Hill, 1959.

HARE, A. P. *Handbook of Small Group Research*. New York: The Free Press of Glencoe, 1962.

HARROWER, G. F., AND COX, K. J. The results obtained from a number of occupational groupings on the professional level with the Rorschach group method. *Bull. Canad. Psych. Assn.*, 2, 1942, 31-33.

HAUSER, H. Journeymen's societies. In *Encyclopedia of the Social Sciences*, 8, 424-427, 1932.

HENDERSON, A. M., AND PARSONS, T. (translation) *The Theory of Social and Economic Organization*. Glencoe, Ill.: The Free Press, 1947.

HENRY, W. E. The business executive: the psycho-dynamics of a social role. *American Journal of Sociology*, 54, 1949, 286-291.

HERZBERG, F., MAUSNER, B., AND SYNDERMAN, B. *The Motivation to Work*. New York: Wiley, 1960.

HICKMAN, C. A., AND KUHN, M. H. *Individuals, Groups, and Economic Behavior*. New York: Dryden, 1956.

HINKLE, L. E., JR. Physical health, mental health, and the corporate environment. In Sayles, L. R., *Individualism and Big Business*. New York: McGraw-Hill, 1963, Chapter 11.

HOLLINGSHEAD, A. B. *Elmtown's Youth*. New York: Wiley, 1949.

HOMANS, G. C. *The Human Group*. New York: Harcourt Brace, 1950.

HOMANS, G. C. Human behavior as exchange. *American Journal of Sociology*, 63, 1958, 597-606.

HOMANS, G. C. *Social Behavior: Its Elementary Forms*. New York: Harcourt Brace, 1961.

HOSELITZ, B. F. The market matrix. In Moore, W. E., and Feldman, A. S. (eds.) *Labor Commitment and Social Change in Developing Areas*. New York: Social Science Research Council, 1960. Chapter 12.

HOWTON, F. W. Work assignment and interpersonal relations in a research organization: some participant observations. *Administrative Science Quarterly*, 7, 1963, 502-520.

HOXIE, R. F. *Trade Unionism in the United States*. New York: Appleton, 1917.

HUGHES, E. C. Work and the self. In Rohrer, J. H., and Serif, M. (eds.) *Social Psychology at the Crossroads*. New York: Harper, 1951.

HUGHES, E. C. The making of a physician. *Human Organization*, 14, Winter, 1956, 21-25.

HUGHES, E. C. The study of occupations. In Merton, R., Broom, L., and Cottrell, L. S., Jr. (eds.) *Sociology Today: Problems and Prospects*. New York: Basic Books, 1959, Chapter 20.

HUGHES, E. C. The professions in society. *Canadian Journal of Economics and Political Science*, 26, 1960, 54-61.

HUGHES, E. C., AND HUGHES, HELEN M. *Where Peoples Meet*. Glencoe, Ill.: The Free Press, 1952.

References

INKELES, A. Industrial man: the relation of status to experience, perception, and value. *American Journal of Sociology*, 66, 1960, 1-31.

JAFFE, A. J., AND STEWARD, C. D. *Manpower Resources and Utilization*. New York: Wiley, 1951.

JAMES, J. Clique organization in a small industrial plant. *Research Studies, State College of Washington*, 19, 1951, 125-130.

JANOWITZ, M. *The Professional Soldier*. New York: The Free Press of Glencoe, 1960.

JAQUES, E. *Measurement of Responsibility*. London: Tavistock, 1956.

JOHNSON, E. H. The stem family and its extensions in modern Japan. Paper presented to American Anthropological Association, 1960. Cited in Greenfield, S. M. Industrialization and the family in sociological theory. *American Journal of Sociology*, 67, 1961, 316.

JONES, H. M. Looking around. *Harvard Business Review*, 31, 1953, 133-142.

KARSH, B., SEIDMAN, J., AND LILIENTHAL, D. M. The union organizer and his tactics, a case study. *American Journal of Sociology*, 59, 1953, 113-122.

KATZ, D., MACCOBY, N., AND MORSE, NANCY C. *Productivity, Supervision, and Morale in an Office Situation*. Ann Arbor, Mich.: Survey Research Center, 1950.

KERR, C. Changing social structures. In Moore, W. E. and Feldman, A. S. (eds.) *Labor Commitment and Social Change in Developing Areas*. New York: Social Science Research Council, 1960, Chapter 19.

KERR, C., DUNLOP, J. T., HARBISON, F. H., AND MYERS, C. A. *Industrialism and Industrial Man*. Cambridge, Mass.: Harvard University Press, 1960.

KERR, C., AND SIEGEL, A. The interindustry propensity to strike — an international comparison. In Kornhauser, A., Dublin, R., and Ross, A. M. (eds.) *Industrial Conflict*. New York: McGraw-Hill, 1954, Chapter 14.

KORNHAUSER, A., DUBIN, R., AND ROSS, A. M. (eds.) *Industrial Conflict*. New York: McGraw-Hill, 1954.

KORNHAUSER, W. (with the assistance of Hagstrom, W. O.) *Scientists in Industry*. Berkeley and Los Angeles: University of California Press, 1962.

KOVNER, J., AND LAHNE, H. J. Shop society and the union. *Industrial and Labor Relations Review*, 7, 1953, 3-14.

KRIESBERG, L. Careers, organization size, and succession. *American Journal of Sociology*, 68, 1962, 355-359.

KRUPP, S. *Pattern in Organization Analysis*. Philadelphia: Chilton, 1961.

LANDSBERGER, H. A. *Hawthorne Revisited: Management and the Worker, Its Critics, and Developments in Human Relations in Industry*. Ithaca, N. Y.: Cornell University Press, 1958.

LARSEN, O. N., AND HILL, R. J., "Social Structure and Interpersonal Communication," *American Journal of Sociology*, 63, 1958, 497-505.

LAWRENCE, P. *The Changing of Organizational Behavior Patterns*. Boston: Harvard University Graduate School of Business Administration, 1958.

LENSKI, G. Status crystallization. *American Sociological Review*, 19, 1954, 405-413.

LENSKI, G. *The Religious Factor*. Garden City, N. Y.: Doubleday, 1963.

LESIEUR, F. G. (ed.) *The Scanlon Plan*. New York: Wiley, 1958.

LEVENSON, B. Bureaucratic succession. In Amitai Etzioni (ed.) *Complex Organizations*, New York: Holt, Rinehart, and Winston, 1961, pp. 362-375.

LEVI-STRAUSS, C. Le principe de réciprocité. In Levi-Strauss, C. *Les Structures Élémentaires de la Parente*. Paris: Presses Universitaires de France, 1949. Chapter V.

LIKERT, R. *New Patterns of Management*. New York: McGraw-Hill, 1961.

LIPSET, S. M. *Agrarian Socialism*. Berkeley and Los Angeles: University of California Press, 1950.

LIPSET, S. M., TROW, M. A., AND COLEMAN, J. S. *Union Democracy*. Glencoe, Ill.: The Free Press, 1956.

LIPSET, S. M. Some social requisites of democracy: economic development and political legitimacy. *American Political Science Review*, 53, 1959, 69-105.

LIPSET, S. M. The political process in trade unions: a theoretical statement. In Galenson, W., and Lipset, S. M. (eds.) *Labor and Trade Unionism*. New York: Wiley, 1960, pp. 216-242.

LIPSET, S. M., AND BENDIX, R. Social mobility and occupational career plans. *American Journal of Sociology*, 57, 1952, 366-374, and 494-504.

LIPSET, S. M., BENDIX, R., AND MALM, F. T. Job plans and entry into the labor market. *Social Forces*, 33, 1955, 224-232.

LIPSET, S. M., AND ROGOFF, N. Class and opportunity in Europe and the United States. *Commentary*, 18, 1954, 562-568.

LIPSET, S. M., AND ZETTERBERG, H. L. A theory of social mobility. In *Transactions of the Third World Congress of Sociology*. London: International Sociological Association, 1956, Vol. 3.

LITWAK, E., AND HYLTON, LYDIA F. Interorganizational analysis: a hypothesis on co-ordinating agencies. *Administrative Science Quarterly*, 6, 1962, 395-420.

LOETHER, H. J. "The Meaning of Work and Adjustment to Retirement," in Shostak, A. B. and Gomberg, W. (eds.), *Blue-Collar World*, Englewood Cliffs, N. J.: Prentice-Hall, 1964, pp. 517-525.

MACAULAY, S. Non-contractual relations in business: a preliminary study. *American Sociological Review*, 28, 1963, 55-67.

MACK, R. W. Ecological patterns in an industrial shop. *Social Forces*, 32, 1954, 351-356.

MAIER, N. A. *Principles of Human Relations*. New York: Wiley, 1952.

MAIER, N. R. F., AND SOLEM, A. R. The contribution of the discussion leader to the quality of group thinking: the effective use of minority opinions. *Human Relations*, 5, 1952, 277-288.

MAIER, N. R. F. *Psychology in Industry*. Boston: Houghton Mifflin, 1955.

MANN, F. C., AND HOFFMAN, L. R. *Automation and the Worker*. New York: Holt-Dryden, 1960.

Manpower Reports of the President and A Report on Manpower Requirements, Resources, Utilization, and Training. Washington, D. C.: U. S. Government Printing Office, 1963, and 1964.

MARCH, J. G., AND SIMON, H. A., with the collaboration of Guetzkow, H. *Organizations*. New York: Wiley, 1958.

MARTIN, N. H., AND STRAUSS, A. L. Patterns of mobility within industrial organizations. *Journal of Business of the University of Chicago*, 29, 1956, 101-110.

MASLOW, A. H. A theory of human motivation. *Psychological Review*, 40, 1943, p. 372.

References

MASLOW, A. H. *Motivation and Personality*. New York: Harper & Row, 1954.

MATTHEWS, T. J. The urban fire station: a sociological analysis of an occupation. Unpublished M.A. thesis, Department of Sociology, Washington State University, 1950.

MAUSS, M. *The Gift*. Glencoe, Ill.: The Free Press, 1954. Translated by I. Cunnison.

MAYO, E. *The Human Problems of an Industrial Civilization*. New York: Macmillan, 1933.

MAYO, E., AND LOMBARD, G. F. F. *Teamwork and Labor Turnover in the Aircraft Industry of Southern California*. Boston: Graduate School of Business Administration, Howard University, 1944.

MAYO, E. *The Social Problems of an Industrial Civilization*. Boston: Graduate School of Business Administration, Harvard University, 1946.

MAYO, E. *The Political Problems of an Industrial Civilization*. Boston: Graduate School of Business Administration, Harvard University, 1947.

MCGREGOR, D. *The Human Side of Enterprise*. New York: McGraw-Hill, 1960.

MCKEAN, E. C. *The Persistence of Small Business: A Study of Unincorporated Enterprise*. Kalamazoo, Mich.: W. E. Upjohn Institute for Community Research, March, 1958.

MEAD, MARGARET. The pattern of leisure in contemporary American culture. *Annals of the American Academy of Political and Social Science*, 313, Sept., 1957, 11-15.

MERTON, R. K. Review of Warner, W. L., and Lunt, P. S. *The Social Life of a Modern Community*. *Survey Graphic*, 31, 1942, 438.

MERTON, R. K., READER, G. C., AND KENDALL, PATRICIA L. *The Student Physician*. Cambridge: Harvard University Press, 1957.

MILLER, D. C., AND FORM, W. H. *Industrial Sociology*. New York: Harper, 1951.

MILLER, G. W., AND YOUNG, J. E. Member participation in the trade union local. *American Journal of Economics and Sociology*, 15, 1955, 31-47.

MILLER, H. P. *Income of the American People*. New York: Wiley, 1955.

MILLS, C. W. *The New Men of Power: America's Labor Leaders*. New York: Harcourt Brace, 1948.

MILLS, C. W. *White Collar*. New York: Oxford, 1951.

MONTAGUE, J. B., JR. Conceptions of the class structure as revealed by samples of English and American boys. *Research Studies, State College of Washington*, 22, 1954, 84-93.

MOORE, W. E. *Industrial Relations and the Social Order*. New York: Macmillan, 1951.

MOORE, W. E. *The Conduct of the Corporation*. New York: Random House, 1962.

MOORE, W. E. *Man, Time, and Society*. New York: Wiley, 1963.

MORE, D. M. Demotion. *Social Problems*, 9, 1962, 213-221.

MORSE, NANCY C., AND WEISS, R. S. The function and meaning of work and the job. *American Sociological Review*, 20, 1955, 191-198.

MUMFORD, L. *The Culture of Cities*. New York: Harcourt Brace, 1938.

National Manpower Council, *Womanpower*. New York: Columbia University Press, 1957.

156

National Opinion Research Center, Jobs and occupations: a popular evaluation, in Bendix, R., and Lipset, S. M. (eds.) *Class, Status, and Power.* Glencoe, Ill.: The Free Press, 1953, pp. 411-426.

NYE, F. I., AND HOFFMAN, LOIS W. *The Employed Mother in America.* Chicago: Rand McNally, 1963.

ORZACK, L. H. Work as a "Central Life Interest" of professionals, *Social Problems*, 7, 1959, 125-132.

PAPPENHEIM, F. *The Alienation of Modern Man.* New York: Monthly Review Press, 1959.

PARSONS, T. A revised analytical approach to the theory of social stratification. In Bendix, R. and Lipset, S. M. (eds.) *Class, Status and Power.* Glencoe, Ill.: The Free Press, 1953, pp. 92-128.

PARSONS, T. Some ingredients of a general theory of formal organization. In Halpin, A. W. (ed.) *Administrative Theory in Education.* Chicago: University of Chicago Midwest Administration Center, 1958. Chapter III.

PARSONS, T., BALES, R. F., AND SHILS, E. A. (eds.) *Working Papers in the Theory of Action.* Glencoe, Ill. The Free Press, 1953.

PARSONS, T., AND SMELSER, N. J. *Economy and Society.* Glencoe, Ill.: The Free Press, 1956.

PELZ, D. C. Influence: a key to effective leadership in the first-line supervisor. *Personnel,* 29, 1952, 209-217.

PERLMAN, S. *A Theory of the Labor Movement.* New York: Kelley, 1949.

PERROW, C. The analysis of goals in complex organizations. *American Sociological Review,* 26, 1961, 854-866.

POPIEL, G. Bureaucracy in the mass industrial union. *American Journal of Economics and Sociology,* 15, 1955, 49-58.

PRESTHUS, R. *The Organizational Society.* New York: Knopf, 1962.

PURCELL, T. V. *The Worker Speaks His Mind on Company and Union.* Cambridge: Harvard University Press, 1953.

RANDLE, C. W. Problems of research and development management. *Harvard Business Review,* 37, 1959, 128-136.

REID, M. G. Distribution of non-money income. In *Studies in Income and Wealth.* New York: National Bureau of Economic Research, 1951, Vol. 13, pp. 125-179.

REISS, A. J., JR. Occupational mobility of professional workers. *American Sociological Review,* 20, 1955, 693-700.

REISSMAN, L. A study of role conceptions in bureaucracy. *Social Forces,* 27, 1949, 305-310.

RIESMAN, D., POTTER, R. J., AND WATSON, JEANNE. Sociability, permissiveness, and equality. *Psychiatry,* 23, 1960, 323-340. (a).

RILEY J. W., JR. (ed.) *The Corporation and Its Publics.* New York: Wiley, 1963.

ROBINSON, H. A., AND CONNORS, R. P. Job satisfaction researches of 1962. *The Personnel and Guidance Journal,* 42, 1963, 136-142.

ROE, A. *The Making of a Scientist.* New York: Dodd Mean, 1952.

ROE, A. *The Psychology of Occupations.* New York: Wiley, 1956.

ROETHLISBERGER, F. J., AND DICKSON, W. J. *Management and the Worker.* Cambridge: Harvard University Press, 1939.

References

ROETHLISBERGER, F. J. The foreman: master and victim of double talk. *Harvard Business Review,* 23, 1945, 283-298.

ROGOFF, N. *Recent Trends in Occupational Mobility.* Glencoe, Ill.: The Free Press, 1953.

ROSE, A. M. *Union Solidarity.* Minneapolis: University of Minnesota Press, 1952.

ROSEN, H., AND ROSEN, R. A. HUDSON. *The Union Member Speaks.* New York: Prentice-Hall, 1955.

ROSEN, S. M., AND ROSEN, LAURA. *Technology and Society.* New York: Macmillan, 1941.

ROSS, A. M. The natural history of the strike. In Kornhauser, A., Dubin, R., and Ross, A. M. (eds.) Industrial Conflict. New York: McGraw-Hill, 1954, pp. 23-36.

ROY, D. F. "Banana time": job satisfaction and informal interaction. *Human Organization,* 18, 1959-60, 158-168.

SAYLES, L. R., AND STRAUSS, G. *The Local Union.* New York: Harper, 1953.

SAYLES, L. R. *Behavior of Industrial Work Groups.* New York: Wiley, 1958.

SCHNEIDER, E. V. *Industrial Sociology.* New York: McGraw-Hill, 1957.

SEASHORE, S. *Group cohesiveness in the industrial work group.* Ann Arbor: Survey Research Center, University of Michigan, 1954.

SEEMAN, M. On the meaning of alienation. *American Sociological Review,* 24, 1959, 783-791.

SELIGMAN, E. R. A. *Two Chapters on the Mediaeval Gilds of England.* Baltimore: American Economic Association, 1887.

SELZNICK, P. *TVA and the Grass Roots.* Berkeley: University of California Press, 1953.

SELZNICK, P. *Leadership in Administration.* Evanston, Ill.: Row, Peterson, 1957.

SILLS, D. L. *The Volunteers.* Glencoe, Ill.: Free Press, 1957.

SIMMEL, G. *The Sociology of Georg Simmel.* (translated by Wolff, K. H.) Glencoe, Ill.: The Free Press, 1950.

SIMON, H. *Administrative Behavior.* New York: Macmillan, 1947.

SIMON, H. A. *Models of Man.* New York: Wiley, 1957.

SIMON, H. A., SMITHBURG, D. W., AND THOMPSON, V. A. *Public Administration,* New York: Knopf, 1950.

SIMPSON, R. L. Vertical and horizontal communication to formal organizations. *Administrative Science Quarterly,* 4, 1959, 188-196.

SINGER, M. Changing craft traditions in India. In Moore, W. E., and Feldman, A. S. (eds.) *Labor Commitment and Social Change in Developing Areas.* New York: Social Science Research Council, 1960. Chapter 14. ....

SPAULDING, C. B. *An Introduction to Industrial Sociology.* San Francisco: Chandler, 1961.

STINCHCOMBE, A. L. Bureaucratic and craft administration of production: a comparative study. *Administrative Science Quarterly,* 4, 1959, 168-187.

STONE, G. P. American sports: play and dis-play. Reprinted in Larrabee, E. and Meyersohn, R. (eds.) *Mass Leisure.* Glencoe, Ill.: The Free Press, 1958.

STRAUSS, G. The changing role of the working supervisor. *Journal of Business of the University of Chicago,* 30, 1957, 202-211.

158

STRAUSS, G., AND SAYLES, L. R. *Personnel*. Englewood Cliffs, N. J.: Prentice-Hall, 1960.

STRAUSS, G. The personality-versus-organization theory. In Sayles, L. R. *Individualism and Big Business*. New York: McGraw-Hill, 1963, Chapter 8.

STRAUSS, G. Professional or employee-oriented: dilemma for engineering unions. *Industrial and Labor Relations Review*, 17, 1964, 519-533.

Survey Research Center. *Big Business from the Viewpoint of the Public*. Ann Arbor, Mich.: University of Michigan Press, 1951.

SUTHERLAND, E. H. (annotated and interpreted) *The Professional Thief*. Chicago: University of Chicago Press, 1937.

TAFT, R. The social grading of occupations in Australia. *British Journal of Sociology*, 4, 1953, 181-187.

TANNENBAUM, A. S. AND KAHN, R. L. *Participation in Union Locals*. Evanston, Ill.: Row, Perterson, 1958.

TANNENBAUM, F. The social function of trade unionism. *Political Science Quarterly*, 62, 1947, 161-194.

TANNENBAUM, F. *Philosophy of Labor*. New York: Knopf, 1951.

THOMPSON, J. D., AND MCEWEN, W. J. Organizational goals and environment: goal-setting as an interaction process. *American Sociological Review*, 23, 1958, 23-31.

THOMPSON, J. D., AND TUDEN, A. Strategies, structures, and processes of organizational decision. In Thompson, J. D. *et al.* (eds.) *Comparative Studies in Administration*. Pittsburgh: University of Pittsburgh Press, 1959, pp. 195-216.

THOMPSON, V. A. *Modern Organization*. New York: Knopf, 1961.

THORNER, I. Pharmacy: the functional significance of an institutional pattern. *Social Forces*, 20, 1942, 321-328.

TILGHER, A. *Work: What It Has Meant to Men Through the Ages*. New York: Harcourt Brace, 1930.

TRIPLETT, N. The dynamogenic factors in pace-making and competition. *American Journal of Psychology*, 9, 1898, 507-533.

TURNER, A. N., AND MICLETTE, AMELIA L. Sources of satisfaction in repetitive work. *Occupational Psychology*, 36, 1962, 215-231.

TURNER, R. H. The Navy disbursing officer as a bureaucrat. *American Sociological Review*, 12, 1947, 342-348.

UDY, S. H., JR. "Bureaucratic" elements in organizations. *American Sociological Review*, 23, 1958, 415-418.

Unionization of clerical and professional workers, 1944. *Monthly Labor Review*, 58, 1944, 1229.

WAGER, L. W., AND PALOLA, E. G. "Miniature Replica Model and its Use in Laboratory Experiments on Complex Organizations." *Social Forces*, 42, 1964, 418-429.

WALKER, C. R. *Steeltown*. New York: Harper, 1950.

WALKER, C. R. *Toward the Automatic Factory*. New Haven: Yale University Press, 1957.

WALKER, C. R., AND GUEST, R. H. *The Man on the Assembly Line*. Cambridge, Mass.: Harvard University Press, 1952. (a).

WALKER, C. R., AND GUEST, R. H. The man on the assembly line. *Harvard Business Review*, 30, May-June, 1952, 71-83. (b).

References

WALKER, C. R., GUEST, R. H., AND TURNER, A. N. *The Foreman on the Assembly Line.* Cambridge, Mass.: Harvard University Press, 1956.

WARDELL, W. I. Limited, marginal, and quasi-practitioners. In Freeman, H. E., Levine S., and Reeder, L. G. (eds.) *Handbook of Medical Sociology.* Englewood Cliffs, N. J.: Prentice-Hall, 1963. Chapter 9.

WARNER, W. L., AND LOW, J. O. *The Social System of the Modern Factory.* New Haven: Yale University Press, 1947.

WARNER, W. L., MEEKER, MARCIA, AND EELS, K. *Social Class in America.* Chicago: Science Research Associates, 1949.

WARNER, W. L., AND ABEGGLEN, J. C. *Occupational Mobility in American Business and Industry, 1928-1952.* Minneapolis: University of Minnesota Press, 1955.

WATSON, G. Morale during unemployment. In Watson, G. (ed.) *Civilian Morale.* Boston: Houghton-Mifflin, 1942.

WATSON, W. B., AND BARTH, E. A. T. "Questionable Assumptions in the Theory of Social Stratification." *Pacific Sociological Review* 7, 1964, 10-16.

WAYS, M. Labor unions are worth the price. *Fortune,* 67, May, 1963, pp. 108-113 and ff.

WEBER, M. *General Economic History.* Glencoe, Ill.: The Free Press, 1950.

WEISS, R. S., AND KAHN, A. L. Definitions of work and occupation. *Social Problems,* 8, 1960, 142-151.

WEST, PATRICIA S. Social mobility among college graduates. In Bendix, R., and Lipset, S. M. (eds.) *Class, Status and Power.* Glencoe, Ill.: The Free Press, 1953, pp. 465-480.

WHISLER, T. L., AND SCHULTZ, G. P. Automation and the management process. *Annals of the American Academy of Political and Social Science,* 340, March, 1962, 81-89.

WHITEHEAD, T. N. *The Industrial Worker.* Cambridge: Harvard University Press, 1938.

WICKESBERG, A. K., AND CRONIN, T. C. Management by task force. *Harvard Business Review,* 40, 1962, 111-118.

WHYTE, W. F. *Human Relations in the Restaurant Industry.* New York: McGraw-Hill, 1948.

WHYTE, W. F. *Pattern for Industrial Peace.* New York: Harper, 1951.

WHYTE, W. F. *Street Corner Society.* Chicago: University of Chicago Press, 1955. Enlarged edition. (a).

WHYTE, W. F. *et al. Money and Motivation.* New York: Harper, 1955. (b).

WHYTE, W. F. Human relations theory: a progress report, *Harvard Business Review,* 34, 1956, 125-132.

WHYTE, W. F. *Man and Organization.* Homewood, Ill.: Richard D. Irwin, 1959.

WHYTE, W. F. *Men at Work.* Homewood, Ill.: Dorsey Press and Richard D. Irwin, 1961.

WHYTE, W. F., AND GARDNER, B. B. The man in the middle: position and problems of the foreman. *Applied Anthropology,* 4, Spring, 1945, 1-28.

WHYTE, W. H., JR. *The Organization Man.* New York: Simon and Schuster, 1956.

WILENSKY, H. A. *Syllabus of Industrial Relations.* Chicago: University of Chicago Press, 1954.

WILENSKY, H. L. *Intellectuals in Labor Unions.* Glencoe, Ill.: The Free Press, 1956.

WILENSKY, H. L., AND EDWARDS, H. The skidder: ideological adjustments of downward mobile workers. *American Sociological Review,* 24, 1959, 215-231.

WILENSKY, H. L. The uneven distribution of leisure: the impact of economic growth on "free time," *Social Problems,* 9, 32-56, Summer, 1961. (a).

WILENSKY, H. L. Orderly careers and social participation: the impact of work history on social integration in the middle class. *American Sociological Review,* 26, 1961, 521-539. (b).

WILLIAMS, JOSEPHINE J. Patients and prejudice: lay attitudes toward women physicians. *American Journal of Sociology,* 51, 1946, 283-287.

WOLFENSTEIN, MARTHA, AND LEITES, N. *Movies: A Psychological Study.* Glencoe: The Free Press, 1950.

WOYTINSKY, W. S. and associates. *Employment and Wages in the United States.* New York: Twentieth Century Fund, 1953.

WRAY, D. E. Marginal men of industry: the foremen. *American Journal of Sociology,* 54, 1949, 298-301.

YODER, D., AND HENEMAN, H. G., JR. *Labor Economics and Industrial Relations.* Cincinnati, Ohio: South-Western Publishing Co., 1959.

YOUNG, M., AND WILLMOTT, P. *Family and Kinship in East London.* Glencoe, Ill.: The Free Press, 1957.

ZALEZNIK, A., CHRISTENSEN, C. R., AND ROETHLISBERGER, F. J., with the assistance and collaboration of Homans, G. C. *The Motivation, Productivity, and Satisfaction of Workers*: A Prediction Study. Boston: Harvard University Division of Research, Graduate School of Business Administration, 1958.

NAME INDEX

163

Name Index

Faris, R. E. L., 34, 80, 151
Faunce, W. A., 47, 75, 151
Fellin, P., 87, 151
Fichlander, T. C., 29, 151
Form, W. H., 38, 77, 84, 115, 151, 156
Foote, N. N., 85, 151
Freud, S., 2, 151
Friedmann, G., 3, 31, 127, 151

Gardner, B. B., 18, 160
Gay, E. F., 12, 152
Geer, Blanche, 72, 148
Goldner, F. H., 28, 152
Gouldner, A. W., 40, 56, 104, 152
Gross, E., 29, 52, 60, 84, 101, 135, 152
Grusky, O., 57, 153
Guest, R. H., 18, 56, 75, 112, 152, 159-160
Gursslin, O. R., 45, 152

Hall, O., 18, 153
Harbison, F. H., 22, 52, 53, 69, 153, 154
Hare, A. P., 131, 153
Harrower, G. F., 91, 153
Henry, W. E., 91, 153
Herzberg, F., 138, 140, 153
Hinkle, L. E., Jr., 144, 153
Hoselitz, B. F., 52, 153
Hickman, C. A., 27, 153
Hill, R. J., 99, 154
Hodge, R. W., 80, 150
Hoffman, L. R., 47, 155
Hoffman, Lois W., 29, 157
Hollingshead, A. B., 81, 153
Homons, G. C., 100, 153
Howton, F. W., 67, 153
Hoxie, R. F., 112, 153
Hughes, E. C., 25, 58, 72, 88, 148, 153
Hughes, Helen M., 25, 153
Hylton, Lydia E., 28, 155

James, J., 100, 154
Jaques, E., 75, 154
Johnson, E. H., 34, 154
Jones, H. M., 27, 154

Kahn, A. L., 3, 6, 160
Kahn, R. L., 116, 159
Karsh, B., 119, 154
Katz, D., 53, 154
Kendall, Patricia L., 72, 156
Kenkel, W. F., 77, 150
Kerr, C., 22, 52, 69, 121, 154
Kornhauser, W., 68, 103, 104, 154

Kouner, J., 114, 154
Kriesberg, L., 58, 154
Kuhn, M. H., 27, 153

Lanne, H. J., 114, 154
Larsen, O. N., 99, 154
Lazarsfeld, P. F., 3, 151
Leites, N., 5, 161
Lesieur, F. G., 136, 154
Leuenson, B., 58, 154
Likert, R., 53, 155
Lilienthal, D. M., 119, 154
Lipset, S. M., 51, 81, 83, 84, 85, 86, 96, 116, 155
Litwak, E., 28, 81, 151, 155
Loether, H. J., 36, 155
Lombard, G. F. F., 100, 156

Maccoby, N., 53, 154
Macaulay, S., 28, 155
Mack, R. W., 100, 155
Maier, N. R. F., 66, 138, 155
Malm, F. T., 81, 155
Malone, M., 105, 148
Mann, F. C., 47, 155
Manpower Reports of the President, 31, 155
Martin, N. H., 90, 155
Maslow, A. H., 138, 139, 155-156
Mathews, T. J., 71, 156
Mausner, B., 140, 153
Mayo, E., 100, 156
McEwen, W. J., 26, 159
McGee, R. J., 43, 104, 149
McGregor, D., 138, 156
McKean, E. C., 33, 156
Mead, Margaret, 4, 156
Means, G. C., 19, 148
Merton, R. K., 40, 72, 156
Miclette, Amelia L., 126, 159
Miller, D. C., 38, 77, 84, 151, 156
Miller G. W., 114, 156
Miller, H. P., 41, 156
Mills, C. W., 111, 117, 120, 156
Montague, J. B., Jr., 86, 156
Moore, W. E., 3, 11, 13, 14, 20, 89, 156
More, D. M., 90, 156
Morse, Nancy C., 2, 3, 53, 154, 156
Mumford, L., 11, 156
Myers, C. A., 22, 52, 53, 69, 153, 154

National Opinion Research Center, 78, 80, 157

164

165

SUBJECT INDEX

167

169

Subject Index

"Nationalist" leaders, 22
Needs, and need-satisfaction, 132, 138, 140
Needs, Maslow's hierarchy, 138
Negroes and occupational stratification, 24-25
Negroes, identity conflict, 17-18
Noncontractual element of business, 28
Normlessness, 15, 16

"Occupational community," 97, 126
Occupational communities, and job satisfaction, 126
Occupational inheritance, 79-80
Occupational perspective and location, 80
Occupational prestige and satisfaction, 125, 126
Occupational structure, impact of automation upon, 46-47
Occupational success, belief in chances for, 86-87
Occupations, stratification of, and moral structures of work, 24
Officials, in labor force, 30
One-industry towns, 37
Originality, in organizations, 146
"Organization man," 61, 139
Organization, protective nature of, 142
Organization size, 57-59
Organization, types of, 63-70
Organization, view of, 49, 133
Organizer, labor, 119
Orientations of scholars, 104
Orientation, of supervisors, and productivity, 53-56, 61
Orientation toward union functions, 116
"Outsiders," 104
Ownership of tools, 41-42

Participation in labor unions, 115
Paternalistic organizations, 63-69-70
Pathological reaction to frustration, 140
"Patriots," 115
Patterns of personality, 91
Pay, occupational, as power phenomenon, 42
Payment in kind, 39
Payments in money, 39-40
Personality and occupation, relation of, 91-94
Personality, detriment to change, 93
Personality, expression of, and opposition to, 139
Personality, functional aspects, 92, 93

Personality in industrial settings, 92-93
Personality of bank employees, 92-93
Personality of scientists, 91
"Personality is organization theory," 138-140
Personality vs. organizations theory, alternatives to, 140-141
Personality vs. organization theory, critique of, 141-146
Personnel man, a product of mechanization, 30
Personnel department, growth of, 59-60
"Pickers and choosers," 115
Piece rates, 129, 130
Piece rate systems, 128, 133
Point-of-crucial-decision, principle of, in career, 88
"Politico," 94
Power, management and labor, 47, 48, 53, 59-60, 61
Power of foreman, and supervisor, 53
Power of supervisor, and supervisors, 54
Power of unions, 113, 121
Power struggles, function of change, 61
Powerlessness, 15-16, 142
Predatory unionism, 112
Pressures on unions for democratic government, 116
Prestige in career selection, 78
Process roles, 66
"Productivity ratios," 80
Productivity, and supervisor's orientation, 53-56, 61
Professional associations, 105
Professional incentives, 105
Professional organizations, 67-69, 105-106
Professional orientation, 18, 54, 94, 103-105
Professional orientation, similarities and differences with bureaucratic orientation, 103
Professional service (role orientation), 94, 104
Professional unions, 105-106
Professional workers, 29, 46, 96
Professionals in industry, 102-106
Professionals in workforce, 102
Profit and legitimation of right to produce and serve, 27
Proprietarial element, in career selection, 80
Proprietors, 30
Putting-out system, 12, 129

170